Hazard and Prospect

Also by Kelly Cherry

POETRY

Rising Venus

Death and Transfiguration

God's Loud Hand

Natural Theology

Relativity: A Point of View

Lovers and Agnostics

FICTION

We Can Still Be Friends

The Society of Friends

My Life and Dr. Joyce Brothers

The Lost Traveller's Dream

In the Wink of an Eye

Augusta Played

Sick and Full of Burning

NONFICTION

History, Passion, Freedom, Death, and Hope: Prose about Poetry

Writing the World

The Exiled Heart: A Meditative Autobiography

LIMITED EDITIONS

The Globe and the Brain, an essay

Welsh Table Talk, poems

An Other Woman, a poem

The Poem, an essay

Time out of Mind, poems

Benjamin John, a poem

Songs for a Soviet Composer, poems

Conversion, a story

TRANSLATION

Antigone, in *Sophocles, 2*

Octavia, in *Seneca: The Tragedies, Volume II*

Kelly Cherry

Hazard and Prospect

NEW AND SELECTED POEMS

 LOUISIANA STATE UNIVERSITY PRESS
BATON ROUGE

This publication is supported in part by an award from the
National Endowment for the Arts.

Published by Louisiana State University Press
Copyright © 2007 by Kelly Cherry
All rights reserved
Manufactured in the United States of America
First printing

Designer: Laura Roubique Gleason
Typeface: Minion Pro
Printer and binder: Thomson-Shore, Inc.

Library of Congress Cataloging-in-Publication Data
Cherry, Kelly.
 Hazard and prospect : new and selected poems / Kelly Cherry.
  p. cm.
 ISBN-13: 978-0-8071-3262-3 (cloth : alk. paper)
 ISBN-13: 978-0-8071-3263-0 (pbk. : alk. paper)
 I. Title.
 PS3553.H357H39 2007
 811'.54—dc22

                                                              2006102961

To My Husband

CONTENTS

I.

The Family

The Family

The father has been killed in an accident during a hunting expedition.

The Mother Speaks

The day they came home without you,
I was teaching Mara to thread the bone needle:
chew leather, I said, the way a giraffe chews grass.

Mara's teeth are strong,
her smile is strong;
she has long lashes.

I teach my daughter the art of survival,
the home-keeping art: sweep spider webs away,
pick the twigs up from the hearth, pray.

Keep a sharp lookout: light is a snake
the color of cream, coiled
in the crotch of a tree; it spits

poison in your eye and you die.

The Brother, a Cripple, Speaks

I was doing my tricks
for the children, beating sticks
with sticks, singing a song
on one note like a bird
with one word: "Me, me, me."

My legs are air but I can't fly.
I sit in the shade of a tree,
plucking my weedy knee.
The children turn somersaults;
sun sticks to their hair like bits of straw.

I used to hunt boar,
my spear tipped with blood,
mud on my back and arms,

a necklace of sworn charms
painted across my breast

with a brush dipped in dung.
I used to hunt elephant. . . .
Elephants shed real tears for their dead,
and during the long drought I once saw a bull cry
silently, as his calves choked on yellow dust like lye.

Children: water the earth with your eye.

The Son Speaks

I remember the air was dry
as earth in summer,
or a cake of wheat baked in ashes—
but my bones were cold;
they froze in my flesh like icicles.

Mother was teaching Mara to sew.
My uncle dozed under the sycamore.

* * *

I have a dog;
his vest is white,
his feet are white;
at night, he curls by the fire,
and his hind legs jerk
in his sleep; does he dream
of chasing rabbits, squirrels?
And you—do you dream?

Uncle says dreamless sleep
is the darkest. I keep
my eyes open,
I prop my lids with my fingers
and prick my skin with the quill

of a porcupine, I swallow sand
so I won't sleep.

All night I walk
to and fro in our cave.
I leave my handprint
on the walls of our cave.
I draw the great deer
on the walls of our cave.
Firelight burns color
into the walls—
red and yellow,
the shape of shadow.
The walls of our cave
secrete beads of moisture;
I will wear a necklace of cold water.

* * *

An extravagance:
my sister will wear earrings
of raindrops.

* * *

Her eyes are as blue as the pool
at the lip of a waterfall
at twilight;
I swim in them
like a fish,
I dive down to dark.
I nap in a bed
of mud and silt
on the floor of my sister's eyes;
I rise on a sun-warmed current
to air, where forsythia
hangs over the bank in bright clumps,
like clumps of light,
dripping petals like water.

I am a willow
growing beside the pool
of my sister's gaze.
My roots sip her sweet springs
and drain her dry.

I weep with my sister's eye.

All That Mara Knows

These are the lessons I have learned by heart: give mandrake
for deep sleep, willow bark for headache;
to chase away nightmares, take
the peony's seeds by mouth.

If your man leaves you, go south.

If food is scarce, feed
on your own tongue;
what words bleed?

The celebrated stone showing my mother's form shows mine:
my stomach is lava,
my breasts are limestone,
my skin is like mica.

My hair is as red as an August poppy—

These lessons I have learned,
but I don't know why I'm loved.
Why am I loved?

My brother sleeps with his head on my shoulder;
my uncle has no legs, but he walks beside me like the wind,
embracing me as a strong wind embraces a tree.

They teach me to dig under the boulder for grubworms and mice;
they teach me where to find wild rice.

I am the student of surpassing brilliance;
I am the first genius.
I live among the cold rocks,
tending our small fire,
cooking bear and deer.
I am learning history
by watching others die.

I know where our souls fly after death:
to the dark shelf that oozes wet salt
at the rear of the cave,
where my father's blind spirit hangs upside down
and harks to the echo
of its own thin cry.

Mara Speaks

I was sewing a shirt of animal skins,
when the hunters returned.
This is the lesson I learned:
the dead are buried sitting up;
the living lie down with one another,
uncle, mother, brother.

Imagining the Past

More difficult than imagining the unknown
is imagining what once you knew,
Boardwalk and Park Avenue,
the pick-up sticks, each the palpable equivalent of a single tick
of the clock
that long, malaiseful hour before Sunday dinner.

In Finland, a woman said to me,
Whatever you lost will come back to you
if it belonged to you.
She had lost her brother, her father, her mother
in Leningrad during the Great Patriotic War.

In that same city, Leningrad,
I last saw the man I always thought
I would marry.
Once upon a time,
I played the piano.
Once upon another time,
I memorized the *Iliad* and lulled myself to sleep at night
silently reciting its rhythms to myself.
He had a Bechstein; he knew Chinese.

When I lived in the hospital for crazy people,
I wrote poetry at night in the psychiatrist's empty office.
A man, not a psychiatrist, said to me, not in the hospital,
I can promise you one thing: no matter how hard you try
to kill yourself,
someday you will have to die.

Who, now, can imagine playing the piano,
having forgotten how to play the piano?
Do you know Greek?
Do you know your brother, or even your lover?
Can you imagine not who you might have been but who you were?
And the man and woman who played pick-up sticks with you,
while the roast was basting—

where are they,
those kindhearted grown-ups?

Her mother is going away now,
perhaps to Leningrad, perhaps to the other side of time,
taking with her all that the child knew
of music and poetry
and Sunday afternoons as impatient as childish sighs.
Her mother is ascending, is flying
upward to light, like Haydn's lark.

A shadow falling everywhere.

Ithaca

I remember a hall of doors
opening and closing. Goldfish
nibbled grainy bits in a glass bowl,
and sunlight stained the walls and floor
like finger paint. I remember
the silence, thick and spongy as bread,
and sound cutting through it like a knife.
Oh, I remember my life then, how
my parents played their violins
half the night, rehearsing, while snow
piled on the sill outside the pane.
Mike was making a model plane;
the baby slept, sucking her thumb.
I used to come home from school late—
detained for misbehavior, or
lost in a reverie on State
Street: *I, Odysseus, having dared*
to hear the sirens' song, my ears
unstopped, have sailed to Ithaca,
where the past survives. Last of all,
I remember dressing for school;
it was still dark outside, but when
the sun rose, it melted the snow.
My galoshes had small brass clasps.

My Mother's Swans

They are crystal and gold,
prismatic and opaque,
gliding across the gentle lake
of her memory as if called
forth or deeply compelled

by that music—that deceptively delicate
music with its urgent undertow
dark as love that lays us low,
pulls us down where its weight
bursts our eardrums like water's weight—

that is its own spindrift, eddy and wake.
When did my dear mother grow old?
I think it may have happened when she was still a child,
sunburnt, sleepy and dream-laden, listening to her south-flying-swans' wings
    playing the lake
like a violin, or later, when, for my father's sake,

she came indoors, took off her outlandish, inflated water-wings,
and put away all childish things—
but not quite. In Richmond,
she smiled as she bought me a feathery white swanlike cloche, and in London,
a wind-up swan that sings

that shadowy theme. Her own swans drift
across the windowsill in a spill of light. They are not wild;
they do not stop at Coole, nor do they light on the lake she knew as a child
or even the lake of her mind. They move continuously, like music, that
    dangerous, irresistible rift
we navigate between rest and rest, art's brave launch and final, balletic lift—

the transcendent, escaping craft.

The Grecian Grace of a White Egret

Child of bayou country,
My mother could not forget
The darkness upon the face
Of the deep, that the sun set

Before it rose, spirited away
By the waving arms of cypress,
That cypresses had knees
And floating logs could grow restless

And crawl up banks.
And she could not forget,
Any more than any lesson of art or history,
The Grecian grace of a white egret,

Its stillness amid the moving mist.
If the death that changes us, changes us
To the forms of our desire,
The wings she wears are not an angel's

And carry her still higher.

Epithalamium

For my parents' Golden Anniversary, 1983

Although he is still surprised
that it has turned out this way
after all the years when
it seemed it wouldn't,

my father loves my mother
so much that there are times when
he is afraid he is going to die
of it, the anxiety,

and there are times when
he thinks that would be a relief,
better than the dis-ease of heart
that awaits him when she goes.

With his arthritic fingers
he threads the needle
she can no longer see
the eye of.

Anniversary

A man and a woman lie down
together, and when they get up,
they leave the imprint of their love
in that place, and it is a kind

of fossil, invisible to
all but the trained eye. The trained eye
spots the fossil and reconstructs
the past, as if a symphony

were to be unraveled from a
single note. The trees of the time
reappear, ringed with light, and the
cardinal returns for a bow.

Encore, encore. Even the man
and the woman return, white-haired
now, complaining of aches and pains,
and they wonder if they need new

glasses, as they take in, first, their
surroundings and then realize
each other's presence, the last man
or woman they had expected

ever to find themselves with, here
at the end of so long a time.

Alzheimer's

He stands at the door, a crazy old man
back from the hospital, his mind rattling
like the suitcase, swinging from his hand,
that contains shaving cream, a piggy bank,
a book he sometimes pretends to read,
his clothes. On the brick wall beside him
roses and columbine slug it out for space, claw the mortar.
The sun is shining, as it does late in the afternoon
in England, after rain.
Sun hardens the house, reifies it,
strikes the iron grillwork like a smithy
and sparks fly off, burning in the bushes—
the rosebushes—
while the white wood trim defines solidity in space.
This is his house. He remembers it as his,
remembers the walkway he built between the front room
and the garage, the rhododendron he planted in back,
the car he used to drive. He remembers himself,
a younger man, in a tweed hat, a man who loved
music. There is no time for that now. No time for music,
the peculiar screeching of strings, the luxurious
fiddling with emotion.
Other things have become more urgent.
Other matters are now of greater import, have more
consequence, must be attended to. The first
thing he must do, now that he is home, is decide who
this woman is, this old, white-haired woman
standing here in the doorway,
welcoming him in.

Prayer for My Father: In Memoriam

After reading Portraits and Elegies *by Gjertrud Schnackenberg,*
in which the poet mourns her dead father

Now that you're gone I find you everywhere:
In poems by strangers, even in the tercets
my students write, art their hopeful prayer.

Yes, you—so single-minded you seemed to care
about your violin more than life's best bets—
are gone. And now I find you everywhere:

At night, by day, even in a sudden air
game-showed during the interval of the Saturday Met's
live broadcast ("Mozart!" is one contestant's prayer).

And yet, I think you were not ever there,
or else why was I calling, calling? Death lets
us draw close, and now I see you everywhere—

omnipresent, like God, both far and near—
and in my mind, you play the late quartets.
To my students who write, for whom art is prayer,

explain that this is art: seeing what is here
or not here, hearing music made of notes like old debts.
You are gone, but now I find you everywhere
in all I write, poetry my prayer.

Miracle and Mystery

Miracle and mystery
    Are swans mated
For the whole of history,
    Their pairing fated.

The bread we cast upon the waters
    Is what they live on.
They are not martyrs,
    Though they dive down

And down, through dark green depths, to find
    Love in the lake.
Their movement ripples the mind.
    They love each other for our sake.

If one dies, the other grieves
    Itself to death.
Two lives,
    One breath.

How We Are Taken

*Lines written while thinking of my recently
deceased parents and what they are missing*

How deeply we are taken by the world
and all its glories—how it draws us in,
until we are surrounded by the pearled
light of late day, the cool transparent rosin
of a clear sky across which the virtuoso
sun (this image reminds me of my father)
has swiftly drawn its fine Italian bow,
espressivo. And breathe—and smell—the rather
romantic, yet classical air. And feel it too—
this world's beauty present to all our senses,
surprising them, like guests who jump out at you
from behind chairs and couches, or like sentences
that draw you in and take you where you never
expected to go and wish you could live forever.

Falling

The air fills up with ghosts—
mother, father,
even dead movie stars (so far past their prime
they're willing to audition, for the role of a lifetime).
And they are like stars,
if also like shadows at night,
a concentration of space,
crumpling of light,
fiery and not quite invisible
(though invisible)
billiard balls of bright spirit
rolling overhead,
underfoot,
until you are afraid to move,
you might step on them they might
trip you up send you falling
down the stairs you
clumsy thing you,
arms and legs all in a scrawl
like handwriting on a wall.

II.

First Marriage

The Bride of Quietness

My husband, when he *was* my husband, possessed
electrifying energy, humor,
the vital heat of violent force compressed . . .
contraries in a controlling frame. Few more

creative and compelling men could fire
the clay I scarcely dared to call my soul.
Shapeless, lacking properties of higher
existence, it was perfect for the mold

he cast me in: classic receptacle,
a thing for use but full of elegance,
an ode to Greece, forever practical,
tellingly patterned with the hunt and dance.

My lines were lies; and yet he seemed to see
aesthetic validation in my form.
I asked him not to draw away from me.
He said he feared he might commit some harm—

some accidental, inadvertent hurt—
and shatter in an instant all the love
he'd poured out in the effort to convert
my ordinary mind to a work of

art. And how he shuddered if I assumed
a new position or a point of view!
As if I were a royal vase entombed
after the ancient style, and the issue

of my movement could only be a change
in where he stood, relative to his wife.
I must perdure inanimate and strange
and still, if he would justify his life.

For I was the object of his most profound
research, the crafty subject of his thesis,

and all I had to do to bring him down
was let my heart break into all those pieces

it ached to break into in any case.
Upon his graduation, when the guests
had gone, and night was settling on his face,
raising my voice above his dreams I confessed

that beauty held no truth for me, nor truth
beauty, but I was made as much of earth
as I had been, barbaric and uncouth,
enjoined to rhythm, shiftings, blood and birth,

and void of principle. He said he'd father
no children. I could hardly help knowing
that he'd be wrong to trust me any farther.
By sunrise it was clear he would be going

soon. Now from time to time I see him here
and there. The shoulders have gone slack, the eyes
conduct a lesser current and I fear
that when they catch me spying, it's no surprise

to him. He always found poetic justice
amusing, and he knows I wait my turn.
The artist dies; but what he wrought will last
forever, when I cradle his cold ashes in this urn.

My Marriage

(Genus: Lepidodendron*)*

It goes under like a spongy log,
soaking up silica.

I love these stony roots
planted in time, these stigmaria,

this scaly graduate
of the school of hard knocks,

these leaf-scarred rocks
like little diamonds.

And the rings! . . . the rings
and cells that show forth

clearly, fixed and candid
as the star in the north.

Giant dragonflies, corals,
the tiny bug-eyed trilobite

grace this paleosite
with shell and wing, cool,

amberstruck exoskeleton,
nice flash of improbability

felled and stuck, past
petrified in present, free

from possibility's hard and arbitrary
demands. Once, seed ferns swooned,

languid as the currents in a lost lagoon,
while warm winds swarmed over the damp earth

like locusts, and rain was manna.
I hold that time still.

Divorce keeps it real and intact,
like a fossil.

From Venice: Letter to an Ex-Husband

(The Horses of San Marco)

I am riding on bronze,
astride a sea-city.
I love my horse
with more than human pity.

His helpless eye,
his cool, wide flank
are no less real than yours,
I frankly think.

His deep gold hue is like liquid,
as if a canal had been poured into the mold
of a horse. He canters
above the world,

bold as the sky,
eternity between his teeth
like a bit.
Oh I love my

horse with more than human
love, with love
that is truer, animalistic,
given to no man.

On him I ride
through salt air and
the sinister, traitorous streets,
sculpture's bride.

First Marriage

I held you, or I never held you, or I held you briefly, once, long ago, and you kissed me while my heart kept time.

Or perhaps not, perhaps it was your heart beating, so hard I mistook it for my own.

But surely the paint was new in the floor-through in the Brooklyn brownstone. And I know there was music.

White walls. Books everywhere . . .

And I remember how the still rooms filled with sun.

You may have taken me into your arms as the music (something by Schoenberg, all twelve tones as sweetly reserved and mysterious as a sundial), beginning in a place of peril and possibility, found its way home.

You may have loved me.

Or perhaps not, perhaps it was my heart beating like a metronome.

Fission

I

The atoms buzz like bees,
splendiferously. Trees
spring into leaf and light
kisses night good-bye.

II

Here's rain and grassblade!
Made for each other—
I seem to see you in shade
and sun, the trickiest weather.

III

A solitary fly
sews the sky around my head,
stitching with invisible thread.
Time is this needle's eye.

IV

You lie, you lie.
I unstopper my veins and drink
my heart dry.
Call me Alice. I shrink.

V

I split. I spin through space at full
tilt, keel, careen, smash, and mushroom
into smoke beside your oaken heart.
Death us does part.

On Looking at an Artwork by My Ex-Husband, after His Death

Such precise measurements of anguish!
The proportionate modeling of protest and despair!
This sculptor welds thought
to air,
finds a material form for the cast of his mind.
But I remember you in bed
next to me, young, your angry words hammering my heart
as though you mistook it for stone. How invisible and unsaid,
forever, that body I slept next to, arm like an armature
beneath my neck, our dreams a hairbreadth
apart. . . . I loved you then and now,
despite that pain, this pain, death.

Wishing I Could Bring You Back and See Things More Clearly This Time Around

(Jonathan Silver, sculptor, d. 1992)

I wish that I could bring you back, and you
would be as young as you were then, excited
about the world and art, and loving to
go on about both with me ready to write it
all down. I was enthralled by every word
you said, on any subject—though not always
agreeing and then you said I hadn't *heard*
you but I had, and I still do, some days,
when a painting speaks to me, or when the world
itself seems like a painting, or a sculpture
you might have made (a thing that can seem hurled
at the viewer, light and shade chiseled to pure
pain, as if pain were what we need to see
and what I failed to see, listening so intently).

III.

For a Composer

At Night Your Mouth

At night your mouth moved over me
like a fox over the earth, skimming
light and low over the rising surfaces of my body,
hugging the horizon against hunters;
or like the other hunted, the one who runs
back exposed like a billboard to the barbed wire and starved dogs,
the men in guard towers, danger sweeping the snow-patched yard
every thirty seconds, the shirt you tore,
to make a tourniquet for your leg, fluttering like a signpost
against the branch of a birch tree, saying THIS WAY:
you were looking for someplace to hide, to crawl into,
a place to lie down in and breathe
or not-breathe until the dogs pulled the hunters past,
fooled by water, wind, snow, or sheer luck,
and I folded myself around you like a hill and a valley,
and the stars in my hair shone only for you,
combed into cold blue and deep red lights,
and the river ran warm as blood under its lid of ice,
and my throat was like an eel pulsing between your palms,
and the air in my blood was tropical, I caught my breath
and held it between my teeth for you
to eat like a root,
there were black grouse in the forest
and the moon on the snow was as gold as your skin
as I remember it shining on Nightingale Lane,
but the dogs' barking in the distance carried too clearly,
a man snapped, STĀT!
and you trembled, troubled and impassioned,
you covered your eyes with your hand,
and I felt the shudder slam like the sea
pummeled by God's fist,
wind-bit waves sizzling against the fiery cliffs of Liepāja—
and you were the ship
the harbor dreams of, the brave husband
the bride awaits, the seed
for which the earth has prepared itself with minerals and salts,
and I folded myself around you like a windrow and a furrow,

and whispered, so no one, not dog or man or man-dog, would
overhear: *Now*
now now now
escape into me.

The Lonely Music

My name is Calliope but some call me Pain,
pronounced like "rain."

I am the lonely music.
I curl on the blue floor like a cat.
I spring from your heart like blood.
The cut flowers echo your mood—

They make a fist and punch air
but I kiss your ear,
knock on wood—
Are you glad I came?

The lonely music lives in you
like a person in a room,
and enters and leaves and returns,
telling you all that she learns:

The touch of a wet leaf, cool
as the scaffolding of a batwing.
In the school of sense, students sing
low notes in the key of grief.

You are the star there, the one who knows
my name: Despair.

I am the music that comes and goes.

From "Songs for a Soviet Composer"

Song of Remembering

I meet you in my mind,
wandering among the cold-swept spaces.
Some faces are forgotten, but never yours.
I have kept you out of harm's way, in old, distant places,
where sleet still spatters a windowpane, the dead are buried in ice,
and a church spire pierces memory traces
as a needle, a vein.

Song about Creation

Trees are the clear bass line;
their leaves, the complication.
Deer are grace notes.
And so forth, if I define creation
as bringing into view what was previously only heard,
God's word.
On the seventh day, he listened to a little night music.

Body Song

Put your mouth on mine
and make music with my windpipe:
my throat is a thirsty flute only sound can slake.

Each heartbeat is a note: draw your art from my body like blood,
teach spine and sinew song,
and play me all night long.

Song for One World

Intricate tapestry, our planet shines,
hanging its cool colors in space. Green shades into blue,
blue becomes water and fills up my cup. My table is a lake, I eat grass,
and carp leap onto my plate. . . . Night is a neap tide, flooding the forest floor,

not deep but wide. I hide in the tops of pines from dark's dull roar.
A new place, this steeple, undrowned, light as granite and graceful as the
    quiet hills,
where people are friends, bound by wind's wild weave.

Song of the Wonderful Surprise

Start with the fact of space; fill it up
with snow. There will be snow in the sky,
snow on the ground, snow in the mysterious courtyards.
You taste snow's tang, smell snow, feel snow on your face.
If you walk forever, you will not come to a place with no snow,
but one day, looking around, you will find
a green apple hanging from a spray of snow.

Song about the Second Creation

Like a stone, sound drops
into being; the waters part,
the waters close; the waves fan out, unfurled.
This is the second creation—not the bone's bright light
that starts and stops, having merely beckoned,
but the one eternity echoes,
love—the sung word flung into the world by God's loud hand.

Song of Time

The years roll down,
like a cataract over rocks.
I wade in shade; the past is a dappled glade.
Time evaporates my tears, and sun—oh, then sun
lights on my shoulder like a bird on a mulberry bush.

Nights, I sleep on wet ground, dreaming the word made flesh.

Appoggiatura

Lover, beloved, hoped-for one, listen:
Away from you, I'm as pale as the moon by day, a winter afternoon.
Antlers glisten in the dying light—deer draw near. I curl up like a snail,
or like drying leaves, lying on the riverbank, my ear to the earth,
    eavesdropping.
Rock's heart beats, gravity sighs; my breath knocks against cold clay; I hear
    death
keeping time until at last the land lies mute. There's sand in my eyes, salt in
    my tears.
I make shale my pillow, sleeping, having hanged my harp upon the willow,
    weeping.

Song with Footnote

Sighing, I puff my soul
into his mouth; the tip of his tongue
is like a blade, and cuts me to the quick.
I lick salt from his lips while he sips tears,
thirsty as a Cossack after a raid. One of us is crying.

This song was not sung.

Berlin: An Epithalamion

In Berlin,
I lived in an attic, crawling
through a space barely big
enough, while
the men below drank
tea and ate hard rolls, arguing
economics. In Warsaw, snow
covered the abandoned tables
like white linen, and my boyfriend's sword on the wall
gleamed like a mounted fish. In Riga,
my boyfriend smoked
French cigarettes and promised
to marry me
and I believed him.
Snow fell in a scattered field
on the dark expanse of his leather jacket
like shrapnel.
I imagined him exploding
inside my body
like a grenade and when I pushed
his head between my legs I felt
I was getting ready to die.
There were people watching us—
there always are,
in cities like those.
Informants, blackmailers—one gets used to them.
In the morning,
he was always gone.
I would watch the sickeningly bright sun banishing the snow from the sill,
the glittery January icicles, no backbone, surrendering,
and turn on my side,
thinking *What will they do to us*
but I already knew the worst
thing they could do
would be nothing. I am
telling you all this
because I want you to
know that even though

love happens over
and over, riddling
our bodies until we are
scarred beyond recognition,
faceless,
and frozen,
I have chosen you
and only you
over all.

The Raiment We Put On

Do you remember? We were in a room
with walls as warm as anybody's breath,
and music wove us on its patterning loom,
the complicated loom of life and death.
Your hands moved over my face like small clouds.
(Rain fell into a river and sank, somewhere.)
I moved among your fingers, brushed by the small crowds
of them, feeling myself known, everywhere,
and in that desperate country so far from here,
I heard you say my name over and over,
your voice threading its way into my ear.
I will spend my days working to discover
the pattern and its meaning, what you meant,
what has been raveled and what has been rent.

Waiting for the End of Time

Behind the window, in that room where rain
and wind were instrumentalists playing
on the windowpane, you were asleep, again,
and never heard the words that I was saying.
I didn't say them for you to hear, I said
them to your heart, that listening, third ear.

What anyone's heart knows is what has been bled
out of it. . . .

   It's February, a different year,
and spring seems something that a season might do
for the sheer delight of being sprung,
a kind of rhythm, a heartbeat, or *parlando*
(the words are spoken even though they're sung),
and everything is different now, except
time itself, which goes right on being kept.

Looking Back

After the revolution

There was this sense of history having out-ironicized
their own ironic sense of it,
a sense of having been somehow betrayed
now that everything they had struggled against for so long
had surrendered, pliant, willing,
good-natured even,
saying *You were right, we*
were wrong,
leaving them victorious and empty-handed,
deprived of their anger.
A cold, hard rain drenched the white metal patio furniture,
and wind swept the abandoned garden.
Brightening in the strange sheen of rain light,
the stone planters squatted, secretive
as household gods,
and the terrified day hurled itself against all the other days
that had preceded it,
like a bird flying into a windowpane
it does not see is there, thinks air.
Already an invisible barrier permanently divided the past
as it had been
from what it was now
seen to have been, blood
mixing with water at the base of the glass.

Memory

These great trees, like towering sad angels,
feathery arms flung outward and down in a stasis of despair.
This stillness of spruces.
This silence.

Like death. Like the enormous absence
that is history, a chronology
that contradicts itself.

Yes, that's right. And just think of the ones you have
forgotten, the substitute teacher
in fourth grade, the friend who was briefly yours
before you betrayed her, or she you.

And the one, that man
you went walking with,
in woods outside Riga,
the green cloud of trees
in the distance, unmoving,
embalmed in memory, if remembered at all.

If not, he was never there.
You were never in that complicated country.
You never saw how the light persevered,
braving its way through massed branches of spruce, birch, and pine
to shine like a lantern, showing

the long way back.

IV.

Lady Macbeth on the Psych Ward

Man on the Hall

There wasn't a single girl who'd not fly off
like a scared wren, but left her dorm room door
open a crack to hear and see what rough
beast was slouching toward the emptied floor,
and when the guy was gone and the all-clear sounded,
we all flew back to ask one another
if he was taken—or was he someone's brother
(which meant *available*)? If dumped, rebounded?
Pre-med? Or law? It was a kind of cooing
we made, we girls with our talk of wooing.

How to imagine now the maddening feeling
of being worth less than a man? The ceiling
's in shards.
         —It was not easy. Our lives bled
on the books we wrote, some you may have read.

Nobody's Fool

Gazing down
that dark well.
A good-looking man pushed me—
in I fell.

Walls of gloom,
stink of damp.
Wish I'd brought
my Coleman lamp.

Down I go,
no moss on my back.
Will it never end?
Will I ever get back?

Wait, here's water,
black as a bruise.
I may take
a long cruise,

I just might choose
to live here forever.
You think I've got
a head full of fever

but let me say this—
nobody fools
a woman who's plumbed
her own depths. (And hell's.)

Lady Macbeth on the Psych Ward

Doctor, I'm lost in these mazy halls that lead nowhere,
sleepwalking through somebody else's nightmare
on Six North, wiping my hands on my hair.

There's blood on my hands, blood in my hair,
blood between my pale scissoring legs where
it pools in my underpants—the fancy pair

I bought for him to watch me wear and not wear.
There is blood everywhere
and I am lost in it. Doctor, I breathe blood, not air.

She Goes to War

Her face is her enemy.
She does battle in the mirror. Look!
This scar dates from Heidelberg,
that one from Saturday night.

There was a Polish boy, son of the ambassador
to Brazil, who carried a sword on the train.
All day long rain broke against the glass
and ran under the track, pooling between ties.

Back home, she lies in bed, scant sun shining
through eucalyptus leaves. Look here,
the deadliest confrontation is the one fought under cover
of camouflage, foliage

stenciled over the breast,
twigs and berries sprouting among the tangled strands
of hair she can do nothing with.
There is a man with a gun and he empties it into her chest.

The Pines without Peer

The pines without peer
Are taller than air.

They grow in the sky,
Their roots in your eye.

And the tops of the pines wave
From the top of the sky, brave

As banners. And the tops
Of the pines are steps

To the high, wheeling
Stars. And your brain is reeling

And the trees are falling,
And you are falling

In a forest, pulled,
Drawn, blinded and mauled,

And you are the ground
And the wound

And the one wild sound.

Dora

    said old
dead things
with her hands,
wings

of
  rough birds
that turn harsh
as words
when you look at

them
     plainly:
Dora's death
is a dull retort
in a short

hard and grained
cold dead
verse of visible
birds of lead.

Paranoia

You're meat and salt,
nine-tenths water; you live on a rock,
craning your neck

to see; you have always felt
something was watching you.
When you wheeled around, birds flew

off, their thin wings tipped with gilt.
Silence blistered the air
like a brush fire.

A snake began to molt
under your heel, full of spite,
while your heart beat

furiously, widening along its longest fault
like California. Now you let it go—
you know

something unseen waits in the green forest,
impersonal and persistent as moss,
hungry as a stalking beast.

Catching Hell

Can anyone help me find
time that is out of my mind?
I can't even remember
who fucked me, or whose member
I sucked, whose book I signed

scrawling my name across the page
as if I were not being eaten up by rage,
my brain being bit
by the ambition-gnat,
feverish with that old contagion.

Whose penis did I squat on,
or want to? This is not one
of your rhetorical questions.
God knows how many sessions
with the doctor, his unclean breath hot on

my neck, haven't brought back
the time I lost when the bottom of the grocery sack
that is my mind fell out.
I should have caught
it; I caught hell. A huge Mack

truck nearly ran over me
when I came to: I was crossing University
against the light.
Next, it was night,
and someone who was not me

rose out of my sleep,
jangling her bracelets, and began to leap
about the room.
I watched her carom
off the wall like a cue ball, I could barely keep

her in my line of sight.
This devil danced all night.
When I woke, time was dead;
it had been killed. That devil had fled.
Time's body bled in the cold bright light.

Bat Mother

A bat flew out of my ear,
saying, *Disappear! Disappear!*
I shut my eyes so no one could see me.
My lashes grew as long as wings.
I became my other self:

Dancing girl, child of surprising good cheer,
full of rage, full of fear,
but hear how she sings
for her supper—eye of newt, wool-wing of bat.
Slip it in her bubbling vat

and never say she never did you a turn,
Mister Anybody. As for me,
I've got a little money to burn
and time on my hands and murder on my mind.
Just let me recollect who it was I killed.

(She was a young woman with a child.)

V.

Life in the Twentieth Century

Family Life in the Twentieth Century

The men go off to war
and come back with the parts of their bodies
screaming like parts of speech.
Leg! Arm! Testicle! Brain!
Their cries are like mortar fire
shelling the cities,
the turning women, restless beside them,
whose dreams are like villages
burning, burning, burning.

The Promise

We thought it had been broken.
In any case, we were sick
Of interminable speeches spoken
By leaders with two faces.
Let them eat feces,

We muttered to ourselves, returning
To our homes. Meanwhile, an army of clouds had begun to mass
Overhead, clouds that rained fire. By the next day, our homes were burning.
Then we lived among ash and rubble.
God's face, too, we thought, was double

And death would come, despite
All assurances otherwise,
But at last we saw a kind of light,
Or many lights: a rainbow. Not like the one after the flood.
A rainbow of blood.

History

It is what, to tell the truth, you sometimes feel
that you have had enough of, though of course
you do not really mean that, since you recall
it well enough to know things could be worse
and probably are going to get that way,
but still want a long and memorable life, which means
having to learn more of it day by day,
the names and dates of all the kings and queens
and those less famous who ruled the territory
known as your heart and now are gone, by one
dark route or another, from the plot of your story.
But you write on, and are your own best Gibbon,
and read on, this monumental subject being
the decline and fall of almost everything.

A Scientific Expedition in Siberia, 1913

From the log

Week One: our expedition slowed,
    Faltered, stopped; we set up
Camp and dug in, but still it snowed
    And snowed, without letup,

Until we thought we'd go insane.
    We literally lost our sense
Of balance, because sky and plain
    Were one omnipresence,

So dazzling white it could blind a man
    Or mesmerize his soul.
We lost sight of the horizon.
    There was one man, a Pole

Named Szymanowski, an expert on plants
    Of the early Pleistocene
Period, who dreamed of giants
    In the earth, swearing he'd seen

Them grow from snow like plants from dirt.
    We said that such dreams were
The price one pays for being expert,
    And laughed, but still he swore,

And still it snowed. The second week
    The ceaseless rush of wind
Was in our heads like ancient Greek,
    A curse upon our kind,

Or say: in our skulls like the drone
    Of bees swarming in a hive.
And we began to know that none,
    Or few, of us would survive.

Secretly, we sought the first signs
    Of sickness in each other,

Reading between the face's lines
      As a spy reads a letter,

But no one complained of fever,
      And suddenly the snow
Quit. You couldn't have proved it ever
      Fell, but for the wild show

Of evidence on the ground. Now
      The lid was lifted, and
Sun set icicled trees aglow
      With flame, a blue sky spanned

The hemisphere, and while we packed
      Our gear, we found we were
Singing, but Szymanowski backed
      Out, silent as the fur

On a fox . . . or the wolfish cur,
      Slinking like a shadow,
That stuck to our pack dogs like a burr.
      Where S. went, God may know,

But we went on to a frozen hill,
      A vast block of the past—
An ice cube for a drink in hell
      (If anything cools that thirst).

Inside, preserved like a fetus
      In formaldehyde, like
Life itself, staring back at us
      The mammoth creature struck

Poses for our cameras; then
      We got busy, and went
To work, and all seemed well for ten
      Days, and then some strange scent,

Not unpleasant, weighted the air,
    Sweet as fruit, and one dog
Stirred, and then another, and where
    I sat, keeping this log,

A steady dripping started up,
    Slowly at first, and then
Faster. I made my palms a cup
    To catch the flow, and when

I lapped the melted snow, I glanced
    Down, and saw how cold
Ground under my boot moved and danced
    In little streams: an old

Fear shook me and I ran to where
    The mammoth stood—freed from
Time and vulnerable to air.
    His curling tusks seemed some

Incredible extravagance,
    A creator's last spree.
His fixed stare held me in a trance,
    His reddish-brown, shaggy

Coat caught the sun like burnished oak,
    But he didn't move: was still
As if he'd been carved from a rock.
    Nothing supernatural

Was going to happen, and I breathed—
    Fresh meat on the hoof!—In
An instant, the pack dogs had covered
    Him like hungry ants spreading

Over a hatching egg, tearing
    Chunks of raw flesh from his side,

Snarling, snapping their jaws, baring
      Fangs that ripped his flank wide

Open. My hands, my boots were spattered
      With blood, and the dogs ate
Him up. That horror performed, we scattered
      Into the world, but late

In the afternoon, I saw a shadow
      At my heel, and I knew
The others were dead—numbed into slow
      Motion, and each a statue

Buried in ice. And then the clouds,
      Piled in the north and east
Like a funeral parlor's stack of shrouds,
      Darkened, sliding southwest,

And it snowed and has never stopped
      Snowing since, and I have
Come with blood in my mouth, my hands sopped
      With red snow, to speak and save.

Forecast

The bombs are not falling yet—
only snow, wet snow, thick snow. Storybook snow.
Yet like most of us, I keep waiting for the bombs.
We know that one day the weatherman will say,
Good morning, America! Dress warmly.
Stay indoors if you can. Try not to drive.
And now for the outlook. Observe
our wonderful satellite photograph:
In this area, we expect a high-pressure area
of MX missiles, and over here, to this side
of the Rockies, something is brewing,
something radioactive. But cheer up.
This is only the outlook. Weather is wonderful;
it can always change. For today,
your typical air masses are cold but stable,
and the SAC umbrella remains furled
in the closet of its silos, underground bases,
and twenty-four-hour sky-watches. Today
we have snow, wet snow, thick snow. Storybook snow.
Today we are going to live happily ever after.

Lt. Col. Valentina Vladimirovna Tereshkova

First woman to orbit the earth, June 16–June 19, 1963

It looked like an apple
or a Christmas orange:
I wanted to eat it.
I could taste the juice
trickling down my throat,
my tongue smarted,
my teeth were chilled.
How sweet those mountains seemed,
how cool and tangy, the Daugava!

What scrawl of history
had sent me so far from home? . . .

When I was a girl in school, comrades,
seemingly lazy as a lizard
sprawled on a rock in Tashkent,
I dreamed of conquest.
My hands tugged at my arms,
I caught flies on my tongue.

Now my soul's as hushed as the Steppes on a winter night;
snow drifts in my brain, something
shifts, sinks, subsides inside,

and some undying pulse hoists my body
like a flag, and sends me up,
like Nureyev.
From my samovar I fill my cup with air,
and it overflows.
Who knows who scatters the bright cloud?

Two days and almost twenty-three hours
I looked at light,
scanning its lines like a book.

My conclusions:

At last I saw the way
time turns,
like a key in a lock,
and night becomes day,
and sun burns away the primeval mist,
and day is, and is not.

Listen, earthmen,
comrades of the soil,
I saw the Black Sea shrink to a drop
of dew and disappear;
I could blot out Mother Russia with my thumb in thin air;
the whole world was nearly not there.

It looked like an apple
or a Christmas orange:
I wanted to eat it.
I thought, It is pleasant to the eyes,
good for food,
and eating it would make men and women wise.

I could taste the juice
trickling down my throat,
my tongue smarted,
my teeth were chilled.
How sweet those mountains seemed,
how cool and tangy, the Daugava!

Death Comes to Those Who Know It

Lines written during the rule of the Colonels

Homer! I said, speaking to the Old One,
things are different now, the trees have thickened,
sunlight is scarcer, Greece grows cool to poets.

Sappho weeps with Alcaeus, Pindar sighs
sadly, and you avert your sightless eyes
while in the distance blind tyranny lies

over the earth like a dark cloud riven with rain.
I think truth will not shine again.
I think this chill deceitful mist had lain

in wait until democracy was done,
and now the sadder among us begin to sicken,
silence shrouds Olympus, and death comes to those who know it.

Report from an Unnamed City

In the square in the center of our city, there flows
unstoppingly a fountain of despair
from which we drink, hoping in this simple way to
acquire immunity to hope, for
hope is the knife that separates us from ourselves.

At night, we gather in small groups
in small, locked houses. Rain ticks against the windowpanes.
A fugitive moon slips from cloud to cloud,
seeking cover. We are still alive,
thank God. Our neighbors have been less lucky—

wiped out, like an insect colony.

At a Russian Writers' Colony

Alive and burning to the end.
    —Pasternak, "It Is Not Seemly"

In all these rooms, the Russians write
their verses, satires, monographs.
A toilet flushes. Distant dogs bark
to one another. Someone laughs—

at the satire! Another someone coughs.
They smoke too much, these Russian writers.
They hack their way through manuscripts
with cigarettes and cigarette lighters.

Their lungs are black as Stalin's moods,
as if a fire, burning the written records
of seventy years, swept through these rooms,
this crematorium of words.

Peredelkino, 1990

A Diminishing Chord Modulating into Nihilism

On a certain day the bombs appeared, like hailstones,
in the sky, massive yet brisk, their falling
creating a kind of music, a diminishing chord
modulating into nihilism and the silence that is sound's
inescapable shadow. This music was so tormentingly sad
one could barely stand to hear it. Dogs and donkeys pretended to hear
    nothing,

as did people, and for a time, it seemed even no *thing*
would acknowledge the vibrations of these new rolling stones.
Yet all the while the bombs were falling, we were feeling, though
    inexpressibly, sad.
We felt as if our own bodies, still upright, were falling
into themselves, collapsing without sound
into an absence of light, like burnt-out stars, of their own accord.

Given this situation, respect must be accorded
all of us who so calmly accepted that nothing
would alter the situation at that point, nothing would reinvent sound
as an art capable of opposing sadness. Angels do not, these days, roll back
    stones
from sepulchers, nor could they, in fact, convert what was, from the sky,
    falling
into anything that might rise. This dearth of resurrections is sad,

but true. (Theologians, who stubbornly celebrate it, nevertheless have sad
faces and are like Christmas packages wrapped in bright paper with dull
    brown cord.)
Therefore, when the bombs began their carefully orchestrated falling
from the sky, they were as perfectly rehearsed as anything
that ever existed, since everything that exists on earth—apples, sparrows,
    hailstones—
falls, sooner or later, and often without making a sound,

but on this day, there was a kind of sound,
and it was a sound like the absence of light, which is to say, a sound so sad
even the animals outside the barn banged their heads against the stone
paddock fence, praying for deafness. We heard chords

never heard before—they were like nothing
in the history of music or the world, these notes falling

from the sky with the bombs falling from the sky, our bodies falling
like scree from a cliff. It was both a merciless and a philharmonic sound,
and the cadenza of its silence lasted until nothing
else lasted. The trusting dogs and innocent donkeys, deeply and unendurably
    saddened,
folded themselves in small places and died listening to those chords
that rang through the cold air as the bombs struck the earth, a kind of
    stoning.

Fallen like prideful angels, we asked, finally, if we ourselves were really any
    different from, say, Muammar Qaddafi or Saddam Hussein . . . or anyone
    else dying to be known. (Something we should have known.)
We sounded one another out, devised Treaties and Accords,
but it was too late. In time, the bombs became their own echoes. *And then
    nothing, not even one sweet, last tone.*

Now the Night

The air loud as an imprecation
and the wind like a fist
in the face, God himself hammering
the rain in like nails,
and who won't hang on,
hang on for dear life?
Something we've done,
something we've done wrong,
the grass flattened, and rain
fleeing into the ditch
by the side of the road.
Now the brief flare of light before nightfall,
sudden as revelation.
Now the night.

In the End

In the end, light gives up the ghost
and atoms swarm, like locusts,
over the fields of sky,
over the highway.

In the end, the air contains
itself, becomes its own jar and lid,
and the stars
are suffocated.

In the end, the air seamlessly seals shut
its own bright rifts, and all that was
becomes indistinguishable
from all that was not.

And the blacktop thruway
nowhere to nowhere,
and the planet like a Chevrolet
spinning its wheels—

Time
takes up its post at the lonely checkpoint
by the ditch,
keeping watch.

There is nothing
but empty highway,
the cicadas chirring,
goldenrod heavy with heat, stubborn, sweating olive trees.

In the end, there is nothing
but a uselessly beautiful planet
wheeling among the stars
like a Chevy Impala.

Requiem

One: Absolute Arguments

All absolute arguments can be argued both ways.
      For example, if someone draws an equivalence
Between his own sufferings and those of victims of the Holocaust,
      There can be no morality,
And if he does not draw an equivalence between his own sufferings
      And those of Holocaust victims,
There can be no morality.

And yet there can be no argument that does not also take into account
      The cardinal that is a small cataract of blood,
The rain falling between branches
      As if weaving itself on the loom of the winter tree,
My memory of you,
      And this: that the knowledge we will die is not forgotten
But not impossible to live with—

A beautiful bird like blood,
      Spilling itself carelessly out of the sky.

I sometimes think there's no such thing, really, as self-pity,
      Since for the sufferer the world does not exist.
(If the world doesn't exist, neither does the self—
      Only the suffering.)
If so, those who attempt to shake someone out of it
      Are mistaken in their approach to the problem,
And what is required is not an argument

But a way to remake the world.
      For example. It was a time, for me, of sadness.
Of endless, paralyzed afternoons deep as secret pools
      That dropped off steeply into night.
—A sadness sharply defined
      By the recent deaths of my parents.

I cannot deny that I awaited both deaths as a liberation
      From various sentences pronounced
Long ago. One is filled
      In spite of oneself with anticipation.

But nothing turns out as expected,
      And in any case, anticipation
Is not all one is filled with.
      Everyone else who used to live here, in this house,
Including the dog,
      Has died.
Nor is all sadness as repetitive and compulsive as a mirror.

I thought that if there were ghosts
      The way they would render themselves invisible
Would be by appearing in forms we thought we knew—
      Mourning doves, or the trembling aspens,
The Norwegian spruce, the pitch pines
      Pining for whatever it was their changed souls had loved
When they were alive as humans. . . .

True suffering obliterates the world.
      To feel sorrow for others is therefore a form of happiness;
To feel sorrow for others is to have been blessed.
      Blessed are those who grieve,
For they shall feel sorrow for others,

As I did, thinking of you in a foreign city,
      Tanks ranked at the barricades.
Or: As I did, watching my mother leave her body,
      And I wanted to call her back
But she was already too far away to hear me,
      Or for me to hear her.
And you didn't make a sound.

You were always self-effacing, a considerate man,
        Wanting not to ask for more than you had a right to,

But from the beginning you knew that there could be no argument
        That did not take into account the cardinal,
As red as a Marxist text,
        And the intricately woven rain,
And my memory of you, which is as absolute
        As both sadness and happiness.
How is it possible to remake the world?

It has been lost, it has spilled itself
        Carelessly out of history,
And how is it possible for us to re-create it?

Is there no God
        Willing to act twice?

I believe
        That if there is a God
It is a God that reveals itself
        As it comes to know itself,
Eternally revealed and eternally unknown.

It is a power and presence
        That must be exactly congruent
With our consciousness of it
        And yet greater, for
The idea is always a projection of the reality and
        If the reality is human consciousness
God must be an idea

Both greater than human consciousness and mapped by it.
        In a poem, Penn Warren writes of "consciousness"
That "loses faith in itself." I mean to speak
        Of consciousness discovering its manifest destiny,

Its belief in itself
     As a fact,
And one that must push us ever onward

Into consequence. Perhaps I don't know how to put this
     Precisely, but perhaps I will. I am trying to know
Things that stay just outside the window
     Of language, and yet the romance of ambiguity
Has never appealed to me, not even when
     My hands trembled,
I was too excited to hold still,

Merely because a man I loved—you,
     In that city—
Had decided to love me back.
     Now rain stitches these black branches with silver.
Yes, and the cardinal is most certainly like a line by Christopher Marlowe,

And I am trying to say
     What I believe, for I believe it is time.
Time to take a stand, and to know where one stands.
     Our parents have disappeared
During the night, wandering aimless with Alzheimer's
     Or kidnapped by one disaster or another, or—if only this!—off on a
         lark forever,

And we are alone, here
     In this haunted, shuddering house, wind
Rising and falling like broken chords outside the window.
     They were so careless, to go away
Like that. . . . Not even a good-bye . . .
     I do not believe that there is a God
That will rescue them or bring them back.

I do not believe in a God
     That can keep those whom we have loved

Safe from life or death.
      I believe that we are so extremely mortal
(And so unprotected)
      That only a God greater than that which I can conceive
Could do that,

But I believe that there is a divinity
      Within us that we kill, and kill again,
And yet it rises, baffled, sad, and loving,
      Returning like the sun,
And we kill it once more,
      And it goes down into death
To be born.

Two: "Beauty Born Out of Its Own Despair"

It was never a child—only a wavelet of blood
      Spilling itself carelessly out of my body—
But I thought of it as a child,
      Or perhaps a very small god,
Something like a miracle, if not actually a miracle
      (Since it died and did not come back,
In any form).

Meanwhile, there were events everywhere—
      Weather, marriages, layoffs.
Anything could happen, but did it matter,
      And if so, to whom?
And what were we going to make of it?
      Under the streetlamps,
The tanks crouched like animals
      Ready to spring.

I wondered whether someone would steal my mother's wedding ring.
      She had asked to have it burned with her.
It was cheap—worn to a thinness, like herself,

But it was a ring, it was gold, why
Waste what wouldn't be missed—

I decided it didn't matter—

I left that house, that lawn
        Where all the trees seemed to be weeping
All the time, and when I locked the door
        Behind me,
I felt as if the past had shut me out.
        The past has no use for us,
Yet—

I returned to America,
        Making that old journey again.

Events are everywhere.

In the corridor a girl was screaming.
        Nurses dragged her to an empty room,
Left her bound and drugged,
        Her blonde bangs in her eyes,
She needed a haircut,
        She needed someone to love her,
She thought she needed to die.

I think about this, about that girl,
        And I don't know what to do.
It is as if we are locked out of the past.
        There is no going back into it
To retrieve what we've forgotten.

History is an idea whose time has come—
        And gone—

And you—but no—you

Are never gone.
            A winter rain as black as bitterness
Gunshots the turrets, which swivel and gleam
            Under the glow of filaments.
People are shouting. A rifle goes off,
            And oh! I am as far away from you
But also as near

As a memory,
            As, for example, the memory of our knowledge
That we will die,
            Permanently. If human consciousness reaches outward
To include whatever it becomes conscious of, a destiny
            In the shape of a universe,
Infinite and bounded,

Then suffering must be absence
            Of memory, and even memory of pain
Is an argument for the existence of God.
            I am trying to be precise
About this: not pain,
            Which is an argument for nothing,
Not even itself,

But memory of pain,
            The way we can choke on remembered smoke
Rising from the camps, the way our minds go numb
            Remembering Siberia, how you fetaled yourself in the snow,
Your knees drawn up to your chest, your fists shoved into your groin
            For warmth, wanting only to go to sleep, and I kept trying
And trying to shake you awake *please God please.*

You had lined your shoes with newspaper,
            I could read the headlines through the holes,

And I was crying, and so angry with you
      For going away like that,
For falling carelessly out of consciousness
      Into that place as dark and dreamless
As Alzheimer's—

And thus, memory of pain
      Is an argument for the existence of
Everything, including you, the rain like a tapestry
      That moves, and the beautiful bird
Like a wound.

For even if it was someone else's past,
      Some other house,
Someone else's door that closed,
      Even if experience is private and nontransferable,
The experience is not the memory,
      Which may be shared, which is like bread to be shared
Among friends, which is like kindness and concern

For one another, the hand stretching across the table
      To offer a cup.

Remember *that*—

Understand *that*—

The smoke, the snow were not our horror,
      But the memory of horror has been handed us
And it is something we must take in.
      After the Holocaust, the two questions are,
Is poetry possible?
      And
What else is there?

But was it not obvious—it was not obvious—
        Why suffering would be the absence of memory. . . .
God, we said—this is the reason—is a presence
        Congruent with our consciousness of it, though also greater,
So that not to be conscious of God is to be out of grace.
        (Here, someone asks if a God that comes to know itself is not
Less than omniscient, therefore less than a God.)

The God that reveals itself
        As it comes to know itself
Possesses limitless knowledge, for the future does not exist
        Until that God exists,
An eternal God creating itself in time.

On the mountain, the light downrushing onto his face—

What is transfigured? Is it the one seen,
        Or the one seeing?
There was a moment when we knew ourselves
        For who we were.
The roses were like red chalices
        Filled with light,
And the sky was as clear as a declaration.

        (Scarcely a cloud in sight—)

You remember, I know you remember,
        This happened only yesterday,
All of it,
        Before we woke to rain,
Blood, fire,
        A new war—
A new poetry—

VI.

Adult Education

Reading, Dreaming, Hiding

You asked me what is the good of reading the Gospels in Greek.
  —Czeslaw Milosz, "Readings"

You were reading. I was dreaming
The color blue. The wind was hiding
In the trees and rain was streaming
Down the window, full of darkness.

Rain was dreaming in the trees. You
Were full of darkness. The wind was streaming
Down the window, the color blue.
I was reading and hiding.

The wind was full of darkness and rain
Was streaming in the trees and down the window.
The color blue was full of darkness, dreaming
In the wind and trees. I was reading you.

Late Afternoon at the Arboretum

Riding along in my automobile,
My baby beside me at the wheel . . .
    —Chuck Berry

The lilacs are in bloom
and the lake that was ice
is water green as crème
de menthe. Flowering Scotch broom

tugs at the eye, Yellow
Brick Road–style. I hold
your hand; your hands, the wheel. . . .
Are we saying hello,

good-bye, something in between?
The car is a Pontiac
station wagon; it's parked
in a very pastoral scene,

and as the sun enflames
the flowers, and the sky
above the arboretum
flares, then dims, making the names

of the trees difficult
to read, I study your face
in profile, now thinking
what dear Ruth had said, exult-

ing in her conscience, to
Naomi: Wherever
you go, I will come along.
        Here amid the alien heather
        and words from an old song,
I say her words, to you.

An Other Woman

The poem of the mind in the act of finding
What will suffice.
    —Wallace Stevens, "Of Modern Poetry"

Text: not a detour, but the flesh at work in a labor of love.
    —Hélène Cixous, "Coming to Writing"

Part One: Waking Alone at Night in Virginia

At night in bed I reach for you, your love.
My hand brushes against an emptiness
Too dark to see; but I feel its sharp edge.
It will cut me if I let it, will wedge
Its way between my knees, kiss me coldly
And leave before I'm through. I'm not sadness' slave,

To let cold darkness live where you have lived.

The room is filled with dreaming moths, and bees
Hang in the spider's web awaiting morning.
I blink my eyes against the unseen room
And tell myself: I'm more than moth, and dream
Of light as you see it, of your warm breath
On my cheek, or your hair lifted now in the car window's breeze.

Part Two: Waking Alone at Night in Virginia, She
Thinks of Him Driving Northeast from Wisconsin
with His Wife and Children

What is the final arrival of which we speak?
Is it that moment when we "squeak, like dolls,
The wished-for words"? Is it that dying time
When, being haunted, the cold gray scattered light
Shuts down, the oboe player puts away
The oboe, and the moon-maddened singer
Walks mute through the garden at last?
                                        Listen,
Those shadowy roses could tell stories of when
Their petals, like oval heart-tipped plates, held
A dust as delicate as cocaine, their sleeping
Stems were heavy with dreams, and the angel of night
Spread out its wings—thick, patterned tapestries
Seed-pearled with stars—then furled them up again
Into the folded, bright hem of the horizon.
I think of you, your life, your humorous eyes
Bluer than the Charioteer's shining
In all that changing, moving, shifting sky. . . .
Your father and sister are dying, they are planning
To leave you, you are driving cross-country
In time to see the changing of the leaves,
Upstate New York at apple time, the road
Home disappearing under your turning tires.
Do I even know the way to New Hampshire?
I dream the distance every night, I wake
With that highway *whirr* in my head, I see
Your face in profile by the glare of passing
Headlights, I feel your loss and if I could
Would reach out to touch you, would take the wheel
While you sleep in back.
                        I can't. Your going
From me always is an inevitable season, is
Only another way of telling time.
Roses are red clocks.
                        Once upon a time,
In Virginia Beach, a soothsayer read
My fortune. It seems that in another life

I had a child, a young daughter accused
Of witchcraft—this was in old New England—
And when they came for her I let them in.
They banged on the door at night, their lanterns
Swaying in blackness, I let them take her,
And it's true I sometimes hear her weeping
In the wind, I remember her adolescent screams,
The grainy grave-dirt raining on her hair,
Which I had washed for her that morning, bending
Her small head under the well-water pump handle.
All these are facts, I'm told, I could not leave
Uncorrected and came back to this world
To amend. At least I mean well, being childless.
Now I wonder: Suppose when you bury
Your father, sister, you should find the bones,
A piece of cloth, belonging to my daughter?
How many bodies does the earth have room for?
Do they touch, secretly under the earth?
Do they hold bony hands, and do they dance
Quietly, or raucously, under their stony crowns?
My mother is afraid of enclosed spaces,
She will not ride in elevators, she
Is unhappy in locked rooms, she will not
Sleep with the window shut. I understand
How she feels, I have been told that sometimes
Our positions in lives are reversed, they say
It's quite possible she was my daughter
Whom I betrayed, we are working these things
Out. Out. Out. Out. Out.
Given time enough, anything is possible,
Even the forgotten assumptions of fathers and daughters.
Even the worst-feared fact, sorrow-bearing
And lethal and powder-white as phencyclidine,
May cast itself in a stunning new form
And what had been an idol be transformed
To living image, as for instance in
The case of the woman who feeds her child
On death, stuffing death down his throat like love.

She's fattening that infant for her table,
She will chew on her baby's bones, and this
Is not a matter of taste, it is a fact
Of ecology. At night, in the dank cellar,
He will sprout eyes like potato eyes, and
His roots will wind through half the house by dawn.
The generations are growing and dying behind
Our backs, beneath our feet.
                                    Your sons will stand
At your father's grave, the coltish wind combing
Their still-blond hair. And as you look from them
To your mother, it will become clear to you
How far you have come and how close you are
Yet; and as you look at her looking down
Into the grave, she abruptly lifts her face.
What you see then must live in my memory
Forever, undelivered and undead.
I see you seeing her fling you away.
You had not thought that she would leave
You so utterly. Her heart is saying:
Husband, and just for this one late moment,
There is no room in that sentence for *son.*
You take her arm, you lead her home.
                                    To New
Hampshire, of course, where I have never been.
I am imagining all this, I could
Be wrong but, *mon amour,* I think that when
You scold your sons, you feel a confusing rush
Of tenderness, as if you would protect
Them from yourself, and as you drive with them
Away from me, your wine-dark wife staring
Silently out the window, remember that
I said those wished-for words, and they were wished for,
Even before you touched me—though also after.

Part Three: While He Is Still on the Road with His
Wife and Children She Receives the Letter He Mailed
before He Left Wisconsin

I

Today I wake knowing that I have read
The last letter from you I'll ever read.
It lies on my table; the sun bleaches
That Wisconsin envelope the color of
Whitewashed villas on Greek islands we'll never
See, the color of Jamesian handkerchiefs,
Bridal veils and classic, ironed sheets,
Or less domestically—avoid that hurt—
The color of itself in August, when
Time narrows to the merest thread, seaming
The sky, and noon's a knot of thirty-weight light.

II

This light troubles and stirs me; I am like
The flower on the table, adjacent to
Your last letter. The power of the light
Pries its petals open, touches, kisses
That unsuspecting face. . . . I yank the cord
To shut it out and still the light steals in
Between the slats, it enters through the cracks
At the tops of the windows, it comes in
Boldly by the door. There is no turning
Away from day. There is no turning back.
The power of the light is this: to shine on black.

III

Black worlds. Stars so dense their great gravity
Swallows their light, they feed on their own fullness.
This is a bad joke, a parody of
Creation. Black holes—the poets love it,
They eat that image and spit it back out
In poems. I love it. I eat and eat, I
Will grow fat with despair, thin with despair,
When I look in the mirror I will see
My own shadow, shaking hands with the me

That is not there, the me that said, "Without you,
I am an imitation of myself."

IV

You wrote, "I am holding you in my mind."
I lie in your memory like a woman in bed.
I remember your unclothed body shining
Gold-red in the late afternoon sunlight lining
The walls like wallpaper, the bed like sheets.
I remember your fitting into me
And the street noises on the other side
Of the window. I remember too much,
I will never be able to forget
Your kissing the back of my neck, the way you wrote
Your name between my legs with your fine pen.

V

For days I have sat at my typewriter
Waiting for words that would not come, the blue
Sky going gray each day at four o'clock.
The rain escapes the clouds at four o'clock,
Splashes the green grass, the cows and bullock
In the pasture, Mt. San Angelo's flock
Of sheep, its cats, dogs, field mice, its bright
Humming fences, Queen Anne's lace, wood, clay, rock.
The grass stalk's shadow lies across the ground
And no words live in my brain, but one sound
I remember: your knock on the door of my heart.

VI

Rain light is thin as pewter; it tames my mood,
I may yet become civilized, I am
Your India, your Africa, your South.
The sun after rain spreads and runs, it draws
Cool shadows on the lawn. Your last letter.
I will bring you bourbon and branch water,

Fan your sweating forehead with palmetto leaves,
Or I would, but I have read, as I say,
Your last letter; it arrived yesterday,
And since then I've not been sure of anything
Except the way the light is sliding from my eyes.

VII

Your father and sister are dying: it's too much
To be borne. They are planning to fly away
At midnight, they will take each other's hand
And leave you, they may go to Samarkand
Or Paradise, it's the same thing in the end.
A tip for the tourist: getting there is *all* the fun.
You are driving east to New England, I
Am in Virginia, your last letter came
From Wisc., and the compass I gave you is whirling
Madly in your desk drawer, it can't keep track
Of all these comings and goings, it's too much.

VIII

I cannot write back—your watchful wife would know.
This was the agreement: to quit without
Complaint, when the time came. Your father meets
The contract better than I can, I am grieving
For the light dying at length over the lawn,
The dusk nibbling on day, the picked-clean bones
Of light littering the flower beds, as if
Jerome had killed it, time being one more
Winged morsel, I am grieving for the way
Night murders memory. You do not think
Of me, dream your martyred mother in mink.

IX

And this is as it was to be, Beethoven
Knew that. The last letter, the light woven
Through the turned blinds, the faded sounds, dusky

As a worn Persian rug, of a piano,
Reaching to the single woman's bedroom.
I think of words I cannot write: *Be brave,*
The world is not what it seems, and the last
Letter is never written, the last poem
Requires daring and tact at the entrance
And heaps ending on ending, when compelled
To stop, it changes direction. It begins.

X

It changes direction. It begins. This is
A woman's way of creating, finding rightnesses
In sudden sounds her throat gives, the final note
Love's cry, a single syllable strung on air,
The rising and falling echo of light.
And in that repetition there occurs
The figure of the man she loved then, and
The one she loves now, and drawing the comb
Through her hair, she rises from the bed,
Remembering where she last read love, the words
She tied around her heart with palest thread.

XI

The end of the journey is a crossroads
By moonlight, the rutted clay gold, the sky
Black as a leech. This is the point where you
Go on and I pour myself a drink and think
About the poem of the mind and body that it must
Conceive, it must contain the intent, must say,
"In my mind I am holding you, my arms
Think you, my thighs spell your name, I am writing
The color of your eyes on the inside of my lids."
This is where you say about me, "I met her
In Chicago and later mailed her my last letter."

The Almost-Baby

It was an almost baby,
inadvertent tissue
unexpected
at this late date,

a mere mouse
of a baby.
We set no bait gates—
they were unnecessary.

The baby dropped down the flue
of my body, dead
as a sparrow.
I love you more than bone loves marrow.

I love you more than God loves sorrow.
Tomorrow
I'll eat toast and think
about you, the way

you slept on top of me,
your lips at my breast,
me smiling, glad and knowing
that my cup was overflowing.

I love you more than
the almost-baby,
more than my populous blood, the well-schooled fish
egging each other on

in their ovarian currents,
diving for air.
I love you more than life
or death, my dear.

Rising Venus

They have it wrong:
I am not young,

was born old enough
to ride the rough

waves of the sea
without drowning, and immodestly.

Semen and seaweed clung
to my hair, hung

on my bare skin
sunstruck and shimmering in

the salt-stunned air.
I had to endure

such heaviness; to push
upward against the rush

of riptide and current.
I said, *I can't*

do this, but I
did it, and I

made it look natural
to float *au naturel,*

easy as the art
of swimming in salt

water, my pelvis fallopian,
eager, the shell scalloped,

the shell's translucent pink
a flat-out Freudian wink.

Did you think that
shell beached itself? That

a breeze as soft
as a hand luffed

my long hair and
breathed me onto land?

And when I reached
shore, I yanked leeches

from my legs, dredged
sand from armpits, cadged

food from scavenging birds.
I learned the words

I would need here.
Learned want, learned fear

and how to live
with both. (How? Forgive

yourself for being mortal.)
Myth is the portal

through which we pass,
becoming human at last,

rising out of dream
and desire to realms

of reality, where love,
a woman, by Jove,

survives, strong and free,
engendering her own destiny.

Adult Ed. 101: Basic Home Repair for Single Women

The Toolbox

should contain utility knife
trouble light
curved-claw hammer
wrench
and rib-joint pliers.

A little putty helps.

Hacksaw and coping saw (coping saw!)
caulking gun
screwdrivers (with orange juice)—

Don't forget those rib-joint pliers.

The Power Drill

is a prerequisite for almost anything
you may wish to do: hang curtains,
pictures of your last lover,
your last lover.

Some Nails

Common ones have a large head, thick shaft. Good for the widest variety of purposes. Box nails are thinner and may be used where the common nail would cause splits. Roofing nails have an extra large head and barbed shaft. The spiral shank of the screw-nail gives it a tenacious grip. Duplex nails are temporary. Do not expect a duplex nail to hold permanently. This is a mistake many women make.

Types of Screws

The two universal slot designs are the straight slot and the Phillips. Both are available in most types of screws. Look for bright steel, dipped, galvanized, brass- or chrome-plated and solid brass screws. Stainless steel screws are also made but they are not always easy to find.

From time to time, you may have to call in a professional.

Painting the Ceiling

Wear goggles and mask when painting the ceiling
or going anywhere your ex-lover may be seen with his new wife.

A roller with a splash shield is also good,
whether you paint with latex
or heart's blood.

Drywall

Studs should be sixteen inches apart
but are often fewer and farther between
and let's face it, you may have seen your last stud.
In that case, use an anchor
in plaster or drywall
and repair minor cracks
by filling the voids.
Feather each coat of spackle into the surrounding area
to help hide the seam.
Soon the surface will be flawless.

Plumbing

The shit goes down the drain.

Class Commencement

Now you can begin
to put your house in order:
caulk your windows against incoming drafts,
drain outside faucets, dig up bulbs.
Prepare your bed.
Clouds are blowing in from the west, over the lake.
Winter is on its way.

Ladies, you are about to find out
just how much really rough
weather
your house can take.

Woman Living Alone

A book on the bed,
radio turned to a classical station.

Raining or not raining, but if it is, the water rushes
into the bushes by the side of the brick house,

bridal wreath bushes, their white flowers
like snow in spring.

If it is not raining,
there may be a blue sky like a blessing

being pronounced over a meal, which,
though taken alone,

tastes of life.

Love

In the attention it pays to each detail,
in its frailty and flexibility,
in the way it seeks out a new trail
while stumbling repeatedly upon the old,

you will know love, and know
that what it cannot fail to do
is render even this late scene
in all its abundance,

the red-tailed hawk overhead,
spongy moss springing from wet bark,
the sound of your own walking
through these autumnal woods.

Work

The old dog, Work, one eye blind as if seeing
wore it out, a limp in his hindquarters,
lies on his stomach on the floor at your slippered feet,
content merely to dream in your presence.

In his old age, the fur on his paws has grown
so long he, too, seems to have on slippers.
When you reach down to rub his wary ears,
he sends you a secret message of gratitude.

Strange to be here so idly, after the days
of long walks, of chasing squirrels and sticks.
The days of hunting down reluctant quarry.
There were many days when he was your one companion.

It is you who should thank him, and so you do,
inwardly. His eyes as they look up at you
are unspoken words; the blind one surely says
love. He rests his muzzle on his paws.

It may snow tonight. The storm windows
muffle the racket of the semis as they speed
past your house toward Illinois; the fire in
the fireplace makes a warm spot on the dog's coat,

you are warmed by both the fire and your dog
while candles burn and the coffee kettle heats.
It is as if your whole house is on fire
with a fire that does not burn or hurt.

This is home, where you and your old dog, Work,
hang out together, especially in autumn,
when the late tomatoes are killed by frost
and smoke from your chimney spirals into night.

My House

First, the hall.

On a wall in a room to the right,
a moon by Magritte hangs from a tree like a leaf.

Birds fly over the pillows.
Sunlight falls downstairs.

The study is small and scumbled with revisions.
My bedroom is not quite masterful.

All night, and the books on their shelves are leaning
toward one another in search of meaning.

Grace

You know of course that you haven't earned it.
For if you had, it would not be what it is:
Beauty of the candle after you've burned it,
the dark bird rising like smoke, always from ashes,
remembrance of heat and light, describing itself
invisibly upon the air of the mind,
that takes the life lived in a fury of self-
love and remakes it into something that shined
so brightly that it might have been a star,
instead of the candle you were burning at both ends.
And now the night grows black, wherever you are,
except for the golden shimmer that descends
to the earth through miles of lonely outer space
and lights up your misspent life, with saving grace.

To a Young Woman

On the occasion of her graduation from Vanderbilt University

The mothers and the fathers mill among magnolias.
Tenderly, the fathers cradle Styrofoam cups
Of coffee in their hands.
                                    The mothers open slick,
Sun-bright umbrellas as the rain begins to fall.
The rain's a soft and slow shower, and whole, single
Drops of it pause, like divers on their diving boards,
Upon the darkening green leaves, the dogwood blooms,
The boles of high-reaching hackberries.
                                                Now, shy ghosts
Of Southern writers are nearly seen before vanishing:
Robert Penn Warren, memorizing three *thousand*
Lines of poetry in his first semester here;
And highbrowed Allen Tate, the great proselytizer
Of all his close friends' poetry; and Cleanth Brooks,
The critic of a generation, Randall Jarrell,
Himself haunted by crueler ghosts.

                                    Almost summer
This far south. In Wisconsin, it was still winter.

The casual rain could be a kind of country song,
A simple tune, something picked out on a dulcimer
Or polished, upright piano, so deliberate
And careful, and the air—the air!—seems vaguely green,
As though dye ran from laundered leaves spread like T-shirts
Against the sky.
                    Your proud father ("Vanderbilt Dad,"
Proclaims a green T-shirt he knew better than to wear
Today) will keep a lookout for your appearance
On stage while also, we admit, trying to read—
Over the squared shoulder of yet another father,
One with a newspaper in his lap—the outcome of
The final game of chess played between Kasparov
And the computer known as Deep Blue.
                                                Magnolia
Blossoms infuse the rain with scent, powerfully,
Delicately—a naturally occurring tea.

I miss the South, its exotic perfumes and palette,
The way one moves through the weather here, wearing it
Next to the freed body like chiffon. (In Wisconsin,
The weather is what moves through you, replacing bones
With icicles.) I miss this world of poetry,
And celebrate your being part of its history
Though you are an Econ. major, shrewder than the rest of us
(But once I wrote a poem about one Mr. John,
Professor of the subject and a lonesome man),
And yesterday evening, when your beaming dad
Draped around your neck the pearls that were our present
To you—small, real pearls—and snapped shut the small gold clasp,
Settling the strand around his princess's clavicle,
I wished that I could tell you that you enter your life
Of work surrounded by love, a rich necklace of love,
Because you do, you know, as do all the others, yes,
You *all*. Say that you are tall and beautiful and
Lesbian, writing poems in New York City. Say
That you are small, intense, a girl in a green dress
Working in a bank to buy time to write poetry.
Or you are the sweetly goofy girl who sleeps through
The first half of every class, or the adventurous
Girl who has found her future in her Jewish past
And plans to emigrate to Israel . . . students
Of mine, young women with the gifts and energy
To save a world, if they could believe it—believe
That love is their companion always, that they are loved,
And they are, and you are, but how hard it can be
To know this, for to know it, you must learn it for
Yourself. And not just once but many times, until
Even if you wanted to forget it—but who
Would ever choose to forget it?—you would not be
Able to, you know it so well that knowing it
Is who you are, it is the subject that is you
Remembering, no longer what is remembered.
Thereby do we create the world in which we live,
A world of love and loving.
                    It can and will be that

For you—in any circumstance—if you will let
Yourself surrender to your own ability
To love. I tell you, there is an economy in this,
The way love returns—and if it does not, if—crazy
Thought, but it occurs—you are quite sure that you are unworthy
Of loving—not only of being loved but of loving—
A thought that can burn the brain beyond recovery—
Read this to rediscover the one truth eternal
As time, which is that kindness is irresistible.
Be kind, and you will find even you love yourself—
That is how irresistible kindness is.
                              It
Has power to compel all things to fly toward
The center, bringing difference into unity—

Power of form, the power to shape and hold a world
As intricate and various as ours, or art
Or reasoning, the power of poetry.

At last we hear your name over the loudspeaker
And when, in cap and gown, you walk across the boards
And change the cap's tassel to the other side (charming!),
We are lifted out of our seats to shout congratulations.
Your father's face is filled with love and admiration.

I so wish that you could see him, see how excited
He is for you—

                    You do, later, amid the mob
Beneath the tent, where parents cheer their suddenly
Grown children—when did they become so formidable
And adult? how could it all happen so fast?—with champagne
And strawberries, but do you know how lovely you are
In your donnish get-up, the pearls blossoming at your throat. . . .

The rain has stopped, the cameras click ceaselessly,
A rain-splotched, folded newspaper lies forgotten on

A folding chair, with scores that nobody thinks to turn
To.
     Commencement programs flutter and scatter like pigeons.
People disperse. . . . Swiftly now, the lawn empties,
Families packing into cars, you are leaving,
We are leaving, sunlight stumbling across the lawn,
The campus left to its dreams of solitude and staying
Up late to study, even economics, the
Flowering dogwood wearing white petals like pearls,
Pearls strewn on grass, the pearls of wisdom, if the will
Matures and gives itself to the idea of
Itself.

VII.

Questions and Answers

The Same Rose

For so long we kept trying to
kill the divine in ourselves
with every possible instrument of destruction,
tangible and intangible,
but the divine kept resurrecting itself
quite in spite of us
(a species blind to the numinous),
so that it began to seem as if
grief and triumph were one and perennial,
petals on the same rose,
or the same rose by other names.

The Rose

A botanical lecture

It's the cup of blood,
the dark drink lovers sip,
the secret food

It's the pulse and elation
of girls on their birthdays,
it's good-byes at the railroad station

It's the murmur of rain,
the blink of daylight
in a still garden, the clink
of crystal; later, the train

pulling out, the white cloth,
apples, pears, and champagne—
good-bye! good-bye!
We'll weep petals, and dry
our tears with thorns

A steep country springs up beyond
the window, with a sky like a pond,

a flood. It's a rush
of bright horror, a burning bush,
night's heart,
the living side of the holy rood

It's the whisper of grace in the martyrs' wood

Sunrise

An egret on the river's edge,
          a sky as blue as if it were
the backdrop for a Renaissance
          view of the Ascension (that slow, sure

stately flight from earthly sorrow
          into Paradise,
where angels patrol
          the hallways of God's highrise,

looking a little like egrets
          themselves, so long and white
and winged), a morning
          risen from the night.

Study for an Annunciation

Mary in thought, though her thoughts are free of sin
even in the sinful quattrocento.
An angel's wing as wide and flat as a fin,
as if the announcing angel swam through blue
sky. This wing so richly outlandish, it could be
the glittering keel of a golden boat steered carefully
to shore, where it transformed itself into
something amphibian, whose words she heard
as if they had risen through miles of water, distant
and parsed into syllables like scuba bubbles
and saying merely what she already knew,
that even the perfect life begins below
and not on high, within the flux, the dreamy
flow that had caught her in its undertow.

Virgin and Child

I'll say that there are bits of gold
        stuck in her hair, star-bits, brilliant
               blue slivers at the edge of the painting
that seem to dance in the light
        from the fire. I'll say there's a fire
               even though there can't be
and I'll say the painting is as large as a room
        and it can be. She moves in it
               as if it is a room,
the gold bits gleaming like candles
        that consume nothing, not even themselves.
               The child crawls out of her arms
and onto the floor
        and his plump wrists
        and knees
are like loaves of bread,
        his mouth smells of milk,
               his palms are so tiny
there's no room for even one nail hole.
        She steps out of the frame,
               her hair sparkling
and the background to everything lapis lazuli and glittering,
        and when she calls to him, clapping
               and laughing,
he hurtles toward her,
        on all fours of course,
               and she catches him up
and swings him over her head,
        and her hair with the stars pinned in it
               and the dancing blue background
slip backward into space
        and it is the child's face
               risen now, looking down,
into her face,
        mother and son
               meeting each other's eyes
as we look on.

Galilee

Suppose another time while walking on water
he grew weary and decided to sit down
upon a wave cresting in a white curve
under the sun, to catch his breath, and fish
swam back and forth around him, silver needles
sewing the sea in a seamless stitchery,
the sun a sequin on the bright bodice of sky,
the anchoring hem of his robe embroidered with salt.

You on the shore! Can you imagine how
you would have felt, knowing that here was a god
at sea, one who had already gotten
his feet wet, one who, though he was not in
over his head, was drifting even then
toward the nakedness of eternity?

The Radical

Think of it: the master a servant.
Getting down on his knees,
washing the feet,
the Achilles' heels and calloused soles,
the secret, shamed places between the toes.

Not the symbolic swipe we see in the movies.
No, the towel getting filthier and filthier, after all the walking
they had done, and perhaps
the weather was not always so good
it had rained, there had been mud
it had not rained, it was extremely hot,
so hot they didn't even piss, residue of salt on their skin so thick
it was nearly geological,
as they crossed from Bethany into Jerusalem
and mixed in the crowded, urgent streets of the city,

which was palmy with spangled sunlight,
bright coins scattered on the buildings' sides.

So much yet to happen! And yet it would happen
and be over seemingly before it had begun,
the way life is,
the way we arrive at our single destination
before we have quite packed,
the bits and pieces of our experience exposed to anyone,
which means that the future is constantly revealing itself as having been
the past all along,

which means that time returns us to ourselves.

(Even if you *thought* you were moving away from yourself,
thought you could outpace that peculiar dialectic . . .)

And now he traces each instep with the nap of the towel
as if it were a country he wants to map,
as if he wants to remember where it has been,

the steps it took
to get here,

the earth it walked on—
to him, a miracle greater than walking on water.

Golgotha

They were scattered on the hillside like stones,
polished by the wind-rag: the smooth, shining bones,
cheekbone and eye socket, the empty skull-cases

of brains that had vanished into various gullets, leaving no traces
of thought, not even a single, stray
idea. For much of that long, painful day

he must have contemplated the meanings of
erosion, mortal decay, vanity, impermanence, rather than love,
until in the lengthening light

that drew on toward—but he would never see it—that night,
he saw—a trick of his blood-blurred eyes, perhaps—them move,
and knew the meaning of the skulls was love

and the one proposition needing no proof
is that God exists because God thinks or is thought of.
God is what remains in the final analysis.

Natural Theology

You read it in the blue wind,
the blue water, the rock spill,
the blue hill

rising like a phoenix from ash. Some mind
makes itself known through the markings of light
on air; where earth rolls, right

comes after, our planet's bright spoor. . . . If you look, you'll find
truth etched on the tree trunk,
the shark's tooth, a shell, a hunk

of root and soil. Study from beginning to end.
Alpha and omega—these are the cirrus alphabet,
the Gnostics' cloudy "so—and yet."

If a tree falls in a forest, a scared hind
leaps, hearing branches break;
you crawl under the log and shake

honey out of a hollow, eggs from a nest, ants from the end
of a stick; resting, you read God's name on the back of a bass
in a blue pool; God grows everywhere, like grass.

How to Wait

First things first: dig in at the lake's edge.
Use sedge for your rug;
sleep on a stone ledge.

No phonographs needed here—
the music you hear is made by a dozen soft tongues
lapping water, by a hungry lion,
deer.

Sun brands your shoulders;
you are singled out for life
by this indelible contact.

Yes, you might as well face facts.
The eyes see you,
the men pity you.
The animals would like to devour you.
No one will save you.

You live by the lake, waiting.
Things to do:

For supper, suck the meat
from a crayfish, or chew watery plants,
spitting out what you can't eat—
it'll feed the white ants
fumbling at your feet.

When the moon comes up, look by its light
for changes—the mountains that move
nearer, the sky that drops,
trees that shed their bark and grow into giants overnight—

The next day, rain.

Locate a thicket to hide in.
Before you enter, make sure it's empty.
That commotion? A cricket.

All day you wait.

You are so damp that beans sprout from your skin,
flowers from your fingertips.
You are budding; open
your mouth to fate
and take it in—
those lips are already smeary with sin.

Generously flick seeds aside.

Grow in the ground; become one
with earth and sun.

Surrender yourself. Evaporate. Abide.

The Horse at Dusk

He was showing himself off,
switching his tail,
thrusting his lovely head over the fence
and a bit put out when I had no sugar
to give him.
Finally, he bent one foreleg against the other
as in a bow.
Sorrel and rapeseed
sparked like the faintest of flames
in a dusk like smoke
and red poppies had ignited singly
here and there,
as if the fire were spreading.
Blue hills stood not far off,
and in the valley
the small lights of houses
came on.
Trees shook their green manes.

The Heart of the World

Each thing in the world has a heart and the world in its entirety also has a heart.
—Rabbi Nachman of Bratzlav

When the clouds gamboled over the blue pasture of sky like newborn lambs patiently licked and smartly nudged by their mother the wind, and cardinals blossomed like red roses on the long trellis of the horizon, and the mountain, still patched with winter white, was like a great cow, say a great cow mooing far off, a sound like separation, plaintive, certainly, and yet expectant because even a cow believes, even if it does not know it believes, that in spite of everything reunion just because it is right must also be possible, the heart of the world, which lives in every living thing and is more easily broken even than the commandments of the Lord our God, which, saith the sages of old, number six hundred thirteen, skipped   a beat.

On Looking at a Yellow Wagon

The yellow wagon,
motionless, in the snow-flowering field,
as a windless day,
seems to say, *Whatever enters*
this manifold scene can become part of it, if you let it,
the way a painting of a landscape grows grassblade by grassblade,
those turbulent bushes
scribbled
or thumbprinted
into the lower-right foreground
almost, but not quite,
excessive.

Questions and Answers

In the beginning was the Word . . .
    —John 1:1

And about the ninth hour Jesus cried with a loud voice, saying, Eli, Eli,
lama sabachthani? that is to say, My God, my God, why hast thou forsaken me?
    —Matthew 27:46

In the beginning is the beginning
and all beginnings, points of darkness becoming
points of light, the pulsing dot of yellow
or red or blue shimmering in the space
where a soul is about to create itself
out of the surrounding unnameable
nothingness. After this stage you can expect
a great silence to descend, like a cloth
dropping over the smooth top of a mahogany table, forever.
This silence is the way you felt when you were a child
and counted inwardly for three days, stopping only to eat,
holding your breath as the numbers mounted higher
and higher and seemed as if they would surely topple
like a tower of blocks, trying to reach
infinity. Or when you stared at the electric clock
(the one with Roman numerals on the kitchen wall),
and you fought back the desire to blink, desperate to catch the minute hand
at the moment of its fatal jumping. All this failure
lies in a heap on the floor of your heart,
scooters with one wheel, blind Teddy bears,
Chinese checkers with two colors incomplete in their triangles,
the new puppy dead on German School Road.
There is always that: the hole in the side
of eternity, through which time leaks into the world,
a plasmic spatter, heart's blood on the hillside,
running off into the gullies like the rain
which is said to have been as dark as ink.
They used to make a fountain pen that was transparent,
so you could see when you needed to fill it again.
Torn pages: you will go to the library and find
that in every book you take down from the shelf
a page has been removed by someone who has
preceded you in the night, and it was precisely
the page for which you were looking, your hand trembling

as you turned to the table of contents. *I always knew,*
she says, *it was ridiculous to say a thing*
like that. Here we will be sorrowful, bitter,
sardonic, and the light that flashes in the brain
like the blue light on a patrol car will turn and turn,
looking down alleys lined with garbage cans,
while rain soaks into the cop's pants legs and he curses
somebody, the night, the anonymous tip, you.
There are mini-rainbows in the oil-slick puddles, luminous
under the cloud-streaked moon. You have made a mental portrait,
pieced from photographs, of her face, her impassive eyes,
her bleached blonde hair, pale white as the pulp of an apple,
and the question is, How are we to step outside
of all these likenesses and dissimilarities
which surround us like a container with no outside?
Did *he* glance startled back at the one who had suddenly recognized him,
disbelieving that the reflection could be greater than the thing reflected?
Did the anxiety in his heart presage an instant when love
would spin away, screwing itself like a tornado
to a vanishing point, leaving only
the vertigo of despair, the giddy view downward to hell,
or was it merely the consequence, the scar, of discovering he had been
from the beginning one who would come after, always after,
a feeling as when you sat in study hall
and carefully pulled against the closing of your notebook's three rings
at the same time you released the spring, but the snap,
when it came, was too loud anyway, and you made a face
as if to disassociate yourself from the event.
You must answer this question. You do not have
all the time in the world. The shadow of the dove
is flickering on the concrete pillar. A bird
like a brushstroke is swerving idiosyncratically
or along unseen lines, dipping
in and out of sight over the sailboat
and glittering water. Have you thought how it will be
when you are no longer present at this window,
and the autumn leaves turn red and yellow
and loosen and swoop and hang-glide even without

you to watch them? The squirrel collecting acorns,
the hiker rounding a curve—what will not go on? You may become
resigned or angry, thinking about this.
What is inevitable is that you should recall
with a clarity so intense that it seems astonishing
in spite of its inevitability
the expression on the face of one man
whom you have loved for so long that loving him and being you
appear to be the same, that loving him
may even be what called you into existence
in the first place, so that who you are, is
an afterthought, but inescapable.
You heard someone saying your name
in the night, and woke with a start,
blinking at the sound which threaded its way
into your brain and heart like Beethoven's
music, feeling created and new. His hands
covered your face and in the darkness of his palms
you lived a million years, every day
of which was like an emerald and a ruby.
What does this mean? What does it mean? What?
That there are portents if you look for them?
This is not a question, and the only possible answer to it
is ambiguous. For the sake of the poem, it is
September in Wisconsin, becoming October,
and the colors are blue and gold and green, with white
clouds which, if the day were colder, you might imagine
were made by God's breath, the Hidden One revealing his presence
in the divine huff, if you believed in God and were not,
as you are, called upon to perform these actions
in a variety of moods, all unanchored by any confirmation.
You know only that you have been abandoned
among twigs, pebbles, grasses, hubcaps, and bits
of broken bottle glass, and the thing you must accomplish,
after your friends have been picked off one by one
by the sniper in the radio tower and dusk has settled
over the construction site, a few shreds of light snagged
on the barbed-wire fence, like pieces of caught cloth, is

forgiveness. This is the hard part. This is the feeling
you were chasing down corridors, the feeling you were seeking to capture
when you sank the dragnet into your mind's depths
and came up with everything but. Here we are thinking of
rejection slips, the KGB, murder.
A man has been nailed to some sticks of wood
and his insides are sagging into his bowels.
Time is swirling around the sparse weeds, eroding
and seeping into the sandy earth, and the question is,
Who is this man? There are holes in his wrists
through which wind roars like wind in a wind tunnel,
and the sound slices into your skull like shrapnel, a fragment
no surgeon will ever be able to excise. It will stay
with you always, that memory of how it felt,
hanging there, pierced, and tied to the crossbeam by leather
thongs. The bad taste in your mouth had nothing to do
with vinegar—it was knowing you had been last, and only
for this. Not the *cross;* that was to be expected.
What was insupportable—what was wholly beyond reason—
was that you were supposed to feel no dismay about it.
No resentment. *None.* It was too much to ask.
It was like the time you looked into the mirror
and discovered that your future and your past were written there,
in minute detail, and the sole way you could revise
a single line was by slowly and painfully
erasing yourself. Later, though you had tried,
the people were staring, they kept looking at you
and laughing, and you didn't know why, but then, in the middle
of the crowd, you saw one man who looked at you
with such tenderness that it confused you, and you lowered your eyes,
blushing, pleased. The valentine box in fifth grade,
lace-edged, crepe-covered cardboard on which red hearts
were pasted, heretofore charged with residual anxiety,
has now been completely transformed by this reassurance
to an object of deep nostalgic affection! And the memories
drift gently down around you, falling like leaves,
until you are walking through your past, each memory
an ash of burnt air, a poker chip, a thin shaving

of sky colored and curled. There was a turn
here, and it has been very subtly made.
We have arrived where we can examine the situation
in its entirety. This is no elephant tusk or ear.
It is the view from all sides simultaneously,
or, to put it another way, it is
the present status of Observatory Drive
as seen from that remembered instant long ago
when you knew you had rounded a curve
and gone on into a lifetime of longing and joy,
though the two were not—or you, being unfond of tension,
were not ready to accept they were—linked.
The football fans are leaning on their horns
and waving flags from tiny Buicks, and
the final question is in sight. *You will
do this or that:* Is this declarative,
or is it a command? *This* is the question.
You will, say, one day go into your parents' bedroom
and discover that no one has slept there for years.
If you lie on the bed, dust will rise from the spread
and sift back through the still air onto your white silk sleeves.
Was this prediction, or did someone send you there,
someone who is not willing to show himself
yet? This *is* the question, this *is* the question.
Things are not so simple, it seems, as certain ones
who have gone before us have suggested:
there are implications everywhere,
whispering in the tops of trees, urgent,
restless, waiting, darting across the ground
just a second before you turn your head,
so you never quite see them, just their shadows,
the light stabilizing itself after the sudden disturbance.
Today's sun has moved on to California, leaving behind
a rose sky that flattens out over the lake, widening into darkness
and deep blue ripples. And now the far shore is gone,
vanished, the island is bleeding into the margin,
and here on the bank the reeds rustle uneasily
in a rising wind, the shed feathers of forgotten sparrows

are stirred, ruffled, and dropped, a large rat
slips into the water—does he touch your foot?
You are surrounded by unseen eyes in the dark,
and the wind has snuffed out the fire in your tin box.
And there are sounds in the forest, there are coals in the campsite pit
not from your pack, still warm, warm as a baby's breath,
and you know that the others, the ones who were
here first, are now hiding not far, only
outside the rim, in the woods beyond the cleared place,
whispering. *Come,* say the voices, *come with us.*
For you will, you know. And they say:
We will go into the unknown together,
drawing the long sentence of ourselves after us,
until only the tip end of it is visible,
a scant bit of blackness, a point, like a period.

And Then

And then a vast, surprising peacefulness
descended, like a blue shadow upon
the snow; and the shadow sleeping on the snow
was a kind of reconciliation, form
embraced by content, light by light, the birds
hanging from the branches like bright red berries.

And then for days, there was nothing to disturb
the beauty of that equilibrium,
which was so like the miracle of forgiveness.

VIII.

Virginia

Byrd's Survey of the Boundary: An Abridgment

Drawn from The History of the Dividing Line Betwixt
Virginia and North Carolina, Run in the Year of Our Lord,
1728, *by William Byrd*

The Prospect

We were again agreeably surprised
with a full prospect
of the mountains.
They discovered themselves
both to the north and south of us.

One of the southern mountains terminated
in a horrible precipice—
that we called
The Despairing Lover's Leap.

It had rained a little in the night,
which dispersed the smoke
and opened this romantic scene
to us.

The Hazards

The bread had begun to grow scanty
and the winter season to advance
apace.

We had likewise reason to apprehend
the consequences of being intercepted
by deep snows
and the swelling of the many waters
between us and home.

About Elk

One of the men picked up a pair of elk's horns.
Rare to find any tokens of those animals
so far to the south.

They are very shy and have
the sense of smelling so exquisite
that they wind a man at a great distance.

They commonly herd together,
and the Indians say if one of the drove
happen by some wound to be disabled
from making his escape,
the rest will forsake their fears
to defend their friend, which
they will do with great obstinacy
till they are
killed
upon the spot.

Though, otherwise,
they are so alarmed at the sight of a man
that to avoid him
they will sometimes throw themselves down
very high
precipices.

The Prospect

In the afternoon we marched up again to the top of the hill
to entertain our eyes a second time
with a view of the mountains,
but a perverse fog
arose.

The Hazards

The rain continued most of the day and some
part of the night, which
incommoded us
much.

The Prospect

In the evening a brisk northwester swept
all the clouds from the sky and exposed
the mountains as well as the stars
to our prospect.

The Hazards

We encamped on Crooked Creek, near
a thicket of canes, though
to our sorrow, firewood was scarce.

About Bear

Our hunters killed two bears,
which made all other misfortunes
easy.
Certainly no Tartar ever loved horseflesh
better than woodsmen do bear.

The truth of it is, it may be proper food for such
as work or ride
it off,
but
(with our chaplain's leave,
who loved it much),
I think it not a very proper diet for saints,
because 'tis apt to make them
a little
rampant.

And now, for the good of mankind and for the better
peopling
an infant colony,
which has no want but that of inhabitants,
I will venture to publish a secret
of importance

which our Indian
disclosed to me.
I asked him the reason why few or none of his countrywomen were barren.
To which question he answered,
with a broad grin upon his face,
they had an infallible secret for that:
If any Indian woman
did not prove with child
at a decent time
after marriage,
the husband,
to save his reputation with the women,
forthwith entered into
a bear diet
for six weeks,
which in that time makes him so vigorous
that he grows exceedingly impertinent
to his poor wife,
and 'tis great odds but he makes her a mother
in nine months.

And thus much I am able to say, besides, for the reputation of the bear diet,
that all the married men of our company were joyful fathers
within forty weeks after they got home,
and most of the single men had children sworn to them
within the same time,
our chaplain always excepted
(who,
with much ado,
made a shift to cast out that
kind of devil
by dint of fasting,
and prayer).

God in the South

settled into the hammock
to read a Good Book,
dozed off,
the book sliding to his side.

The sun rose to its full height,
a tall light bending
over the sleeping God,

over a rose climbing a trellis,
a child scolding her doll
then saying, "I forgive you,"

over a piece of blue cloth
snagged on the splintering fence,

scrap of fallen sky
doll's dress
or God's dream.

God's Picnic (Blue Ridge)

God takes a left
off the Skyline Drive,
parks at a Scenic View,
picks out a rock,
unpacks a picnic.

The valley is a hammock strung between mountains.

He chews while gazing at the panorama.
Later, he drives back to his motel,
nearly empty off season,
enters his room to write a poem
about the state of his creation.

The Garden

In the cool of the evening
the wind roused itself
and went walking
in the garden. Leaves
let go of trees,
dropping to the ground
with a slight, agreeable sound.
The petals of pinks
floated in the wind's hands
like small boats.
The moon was round
as an apple and stars
salted the sky.
Where were Adam and Eve?
Nowhere to be found.
Fireflies lighted lanterns
as the dewed grasses nodded;
as ferns, modest in their mantillas,
waited on the sidelines;
as a mockingbird
relinquished irony and fell silent.
The humans arrived,
dressed in shame,
and the wind sighed
and twistered them
out of paradise.
Then the wind died,
leaving the garden to grow
wild as wild horses.

In the Field

The kind of day
when everything is so still
it seems to be an image of itself,
a mirrored photograph,
and only the secret lives of insects,
intense and determined among the leaves and grass,
enact the motivations of the real.

In this shadowless light
of uncontaminated noon, a fence post
gleams as if gilded, church spire where there is no church.
The impossibly beautiful blossoms of the crab apple
have spilled onto the ground,
an imperturbable pool of pink and white.
This illusion of the real, almost real.

Wild Dogwood

1

Her betrothed had brought her
a bloom. The mountain was mad with it,
the froth and foam of it. He tucked
the bloom behind her ear and smoothed
her hair over the stem.
                              Sometimes,
when he's not there,
when he takes his rig to
Atlanta or Birmingham,
she pushes aside the book
she has been reading and walks
on the mountain in moonlight,
stopping under the poplars and the pines to watch
the wind pulling at white petals
like a girl asking a daisy
if he loves her or loves her not.

2

The wild dogwoods are dying.
The bright, tumbling clouds of them are disappearing.

A breath blown into history.

Blue Jay

I saw a blue jay
in the cedar tree today.
He soon flew off
to a farther spot
where holly trees grow dark
starry leaves beside the tool shed,
fanning stylish wings
as he settled down,
safe for the duration.

Tonight, with sudden weather
homing in on
our small part of the state,
I think again about
the startle of his tail,
the reaching art
that took him here to there.

The Shape of the Air

It was raining goldfinches.
    Pouring like water,
they filled the lawn with light
    bright as bullion.

And then they vanished,
    a stream rushing down the sky.
The light left; the coolness of their small storm left.
    We'd only memory to see them by.

Must beauty be sudden and short,
    a surprise that dies?
Or is beauty the shape of the air
    after finches fly?

The Heat Down South (Richmond, 1955)

The heat does something wonderful
and difficult for Northerners to grasp.
It says a silent benediction,
it houses us in torpor.
A halo of humidity
surrounds the porch, the people
are robed in sweat and none contrive
to do much more than read a magazine.
To turn the fan to "on" is strenuous
and so is reaching for a beer. Night
may bring relief or trouble but
tonight's forever from now.
A six-foot floor-fan shuffles the air,
which doesn't cool the room,
and no one stirs, and nothing else
is moving. Telephones won't ring:
Forget the will to power,
we haven't the will to say hello.
No one knocks. You are secured
from all assaults upon your consciousness
and there is nothing to keep you from
imagining a wiser nation might
arise among the fields and woods,
the birds at liberty,
the lions lying down with lambs.

A Farm in Virginia near the North Carolina Boundary

The shadow of a grassblade falls upon the worm.
A blue-tailed skink slips in under the door.
This is life as lived on a southern farm
with fruit trees (apple orchard; fig and pear).
Scarlet tanagers let themselves be seen
from time to time. Rabbits and deer devour
the season's garden. Bees linger at the screen.
Some days the sky is low and seems to lower,
and others blue, with clouds a rickrack trim,
or black with blowing rain that stills and hushes
the birds while large-mouth bass and turtles swim
in the muddy-bottomed pond; rain rattles bushes.
It's busy here; a lot is going on
most all the time and now and then scarlet
tanagers, bright baubles in the morning sun,
and shy despite the gaudy garb of harlot,
fly by, a pair; house wrens flock at the feeder.
The bees that fumble at the sill will swarm.
A cardinal relaxes in a cedar.
This is life on a small southeastern farm.
A blue-tailed skink slips out under the door.
The shadow of a grassblade crosses the worm.

Joy

You could be doing anything,
arranging dahlias in a vase,
sipping tea on a screened-in porch,
or sticking stars on fourth-grade papers.
But *anything:* you could be driving
a truck, offloading supplies, on foot
patrol in Baghdad or halfway
to Damascus. You might be having
a baby, break, or second thoughts,
or words with your troublesome teenage son.
You could be anywhere, at home,
at work, or off on vacation.
The flowers may remind you of
Fourth of July firecrackers.
You may recall a day you spent
learning to identify the ferns
and mosses in Pocahontas Park—
a windy day, warm and brilliant,
rampant leaves spinning against the sky.
Or if not that, a difficult meeting
in which you gripped your water glass
tight, feeling the cold enter
your skin. There was the closing of
a deal, a forklift on the dock,
a medical emergency,
a war, divorce, the isolation
room, a glass vase of dahlias.
You could have been anywhere, you could
be there now, you could be *anywhere,*
walking through woods or sitting on
a screened-in porch, writing a poem—

and there you are, surprised by it.

Virginia Reel

At Mayfield

THE GRASS was in bloom like a purple cloud, wind shirring the hayfield, and a picket fence embraced the house, and a small dog barked at the noise of pecans falling on a tin roof. Things must be named to be sung, and the name of the house is Mayfield.

THE DAY was windy and I felt as if it might catch me up, blow my blue skirt over my head and I would find myself, after a whirlwind trip and a bumpy landing, in a green place, with a small dog at my heels and a wizard for a husband, a man who knows the meaning of a watch, the value of a medal, and what words on paper can do.

PURPLE-TOP GRASS bowed before the wind. Lizards and beetles clung to safe places between planks or rocks. Our dog, small and white, was fluffed up by the wind as if he had been blow-dried. My sister, so far from here, was as far away as childhood. Our parents and their brothers and sisters, who had been on the earth for a while, now were gone. We, too, would bow and be blown, like milkweed or wild grass seed, the purple-top grass.

ALL THINGS dance. The sun and moon dance, galaxies dance, the small foxes in the field and all birds dance. The oceans dance, as do the hills and all the flowers that grow thereon. Light dances with dark, and death shakes a leg with life. Time lifts us up and swings us out and back and over. The wind dances with the pines and the purple-top grass.

SILENCE DANCES, it dances with sounds: the falling pecans, the dog's bark, the blue jays' squawk, the tree frogs' colloquy, the constant plainchant of cicadas.

WIND BLEW the purple-top grass backward like a dancer dipping his partner. Wind blew the butterflies around and around, figures on a mobile but there was no mobile. A blue-tailed skink slipped between painted planks of the front porch. My husband called the dog, who bounded toward him.

I shall show you happiness, contentment. Without descriptions, how will we know these things when we encounter them? How else remember them?

We go into the tenebrous forest or the crowded city and are lost there for years on end, searching for what we already possess. We go into the world hoping to close the rift in ourselves, and soul is cut off from self. Tragedy and terror haunt the world, and everywhere people weep.

In the public houses and private byways, we seek whom we love, we seek to be found. In plazas and cafés, we hunt and are brought down.

Consciousness slides over the self like a tectonic plate, sometimes congruent and unbroken, sometimes shuddering along fault lines. To be human is to be shaken, and struggling to remain upright.

AS FOR THE memory of happiness: Some say it is seasoned with sorrow, but we say that gratitude makes mild the bitter herb.

AS FOR THE butterflies: Among the butterflies were indigo swallowtails, tiger swallowtails, ink-black swallowtails, and fritillaries with disks like mirrors on their wings. The dazzling silver skipper carries the sky on his back.

AS FOR THE morning: The morning of the day was so bright it seemed to be shining with intelligence.

AS FOR TIME: Time is the mystery at the center of all things.

MY SKIRT is sky-blue. The thin cotton of it slides against my skin, making me feel young again. Do you remember what your body felt like then, how light and free and new? After all, it had not been lived in long; it was still unused and willing. And its covering was so smooth, fitting your body perfectly, as if custom-made by the Tailor of tailors.

THE PECANS dropped down on the tin roof with a noise like rifle shots. The ground was pockmarked with small pits made by Galas and Winesaps. A plant in a pot turned over on the deck.

My husband reads Faulkner and physics, works in the garden, and puts his faith in facts.

Fact: Time has a shape.

Fact: Our time lies in the blind spot of somebody else's time.

THEORY: Spacetime at Mayfield has curved and slowed.

AT NIGHT, in bed, his arms shelter me. Even after we turn away from each other, we carry the feeling into our dreams. It is the feeling of being home. He is where I live, and I am where he lives.

AT NIGHT, in bed, we hear Little Polecat Creek run lively in its bed.

IS HAPPINESS an accident, a random event in a random universe? Perhaps happiness happens haphazardly.

WHEN MY husband goes outside without him, our dog curls up on the floor by the door, waiting for his beloved's return.

I will get down on the floor, curl up with him. Together we will wait for our beloved's return.

Waiting

THE DAY was windy and the tops of pine trees swayed, and the scarlet oaks stood tall. Apples and pecans fell from wind-raked branches. The sky was bright blue. My skirt was light blue. The wind chimes danced and sang.

HURRY, I want to tell him. Make haste, like the antlered deer that stands in the field, turning his great head, alert.

The deer's eyes are as dark as tar. His horns are like towers.

He leaps, and pours into the woods where two does await.

I await my husband. If it were summer he would be gathering blackberries from overgrown bushes. Today he is building or fishing or stacking firewood against winter. Make haste, make haste.

THE WIND blew my blue skirt against my legs. I righted the spilled plant and brought it out of the wind. I pulled wet clothes from the washer and carried them outside to pin to the line. Our dog barked at the flapping sheets as if to herd them. Then he ran off, following my husband's trail to the pond.

FISH DANCE a fish-dance in the pond. Large-mouth bass lay eggs in the pond's shallows. The elders hover above the eggs. They fan them with their fins to keep the water fresh; they guard against reivers. A rotting dock juts just past the sedge grass and a patch of cattails. On the far side of the pond a heron steps judiciously along the edge of the bank. He stops mid-motion, still as a photograph of himself. The pond is idling, barely a ripple. His beak strikes the surface like a thrown knife. He tosses his head once, twice, to lodge the fish in the back of his throat; then he tilts his head back farther, beak skyward, and with a single gulp he bolts it down. He will preen for a long time before he flies away.

The day was windy. The trees knocked heads as they bent this way and that. Above them the nearly clear blue sky was a language I didn't know how to read. I picked up the basket and went back inside.

MY SISTER is coming to visit. She will stay in the guest cottage, a remodeled corncrib. She will look out the east window, past the shade of a fig tree that splays into a shower of branches, onto the meadow bordered by woods. Deep in the woods Little Polecat Creek truckles along, quietly laughing, as if remembering a joke. There will be birdsong, the chatter of upside-down nuthatches, hooded juncos like talkative friars, and in the distance, doves, those soft gray gloves, mourning.

WHAT SHALL we do for my little sister? Already, she is as thin as she was at twelve. Hurry, I have begged her, come soon! Make haste!

IN A ROW on the kitchen sill are large tomatoes that look like small, setting suns.

MY HUSBAND came back in to fetch the box of live worms that he stores in the refrigerator. He names the worms. He says it gives them the dignity they deserve, before they leave this earth. Fred, Gertrude, Brittany—gone to glory.

HE COMFORTS me with apples, Gala, Winesap. He courts me with figs, sweet-smelling grapes, pears like cellos or Willendorf Venuses. I admired his fruit.

In July we got up early to pick blackberries. He kissed me in the grape arbor. The taste of his mouth is better to me than the taste of Shiraz.

Roses and daylilies bloomed. We lay down, my beloved and I, on the ground, our green bed.

A wind came into the garden. It was like a god, a presence we could feel but not see.

HE IS MY friend, my spouse.

Sometimes I spend the day in pajama bottoms and a flannel shirt. I wear sweat socks in winter when the floorboards are cold. I go barefoot in summer. And sometimes I put on a skirt of thin cotton, a pale yellow top, and then I anoint myself with perfume. He has a hole in his sweater, paint on his pants, and mud on his shoes, and he stood in the doorway of the barn, looking forth. I went to him and his shadow sheltered me while I tasted his sweet fruit.

Time blazed past us like a comet.

REMEMBER HOW the song of cicadas accompanied your childhood summers, how it was woven into the texture of them. An endless song for endless days. They are still singing, if we listen, their rapid, blurred clicking, their drawn-out whirring, like held notes.

A WIND came into the garden.

MY HUSBAND drove off with our dog.

It was a windy day, the rush of it a river smashing through the hay, bending the purple tops of the purple-top grass.

I watched them go down the dirt lane, past the apple trees.

At the hardware store, the pharmacy, the post office, the bank, they shop, refill, mail, and save. They check out used boats at yard sales and pie safes at country auctions. Sometimes they just ride around, and the wind blows on their faces.

Time went with them, the unseen passenger.

This is not like love in my youth. It is deep and broad. It is love like a pond that accommodates different kinds of life, that makes room for all of it.

He is mine, and I am his: and our dog is ours, but mostly his.

My Husband

HE IS my friend, my spouse.

Although he'd rather not, he slows his pace so I can keep up with him.

He supplies the word I am looking for.

When I am standing next to him in the kitchen, he takes two dog treats from their box and places one on each of my shoulders. "Don't move," he says, "or they'll fall off."

HE IS brother to my soul.

HE IS a brother to my sister, my sister who as a child lived to dance. When she danced, she rose from the floor, resting in air. She leapt and whirled to the Firebird Suite. In her red tutu she was a rising and falling flame. I tell my husband these things about her.

ONCE AS I stood looking out over the kitchen sink at the pear tree, the fig tree, the tool shed, and the vegetable garden—and the sky covering it all with blue wings spread and sheltering—he came up behind me and propped a fist on top of my head. He tapped the top of his fist lightly with his other fist, and spread fingers down both sides of my hair. It felt like yolk dripping.

HE TELLS me about stars and lizards, clouds and crops, and Faulkner and physics. He brakes for box turtles.

MY HUSBAND will touch his nose with one hand while guiding his coffee cup toward it with the other; then he'll open his mouth with the first hand and tip the cup toward it with the other; then he'll use his first hand to turn his nose to the right and his other hand to move the coffee cup in the same direction, following his compass of nose, thence to set the cup down.

    He reminds me of my father.

HE IS my beloved and my friend.

HE IS the strongest and loveliest of men, with his new left leg set upon a socket of titanium. Once again he can lie on his side to hold me through the night.

A PANTS-HANGER lay misplaced and lonesome on the dining-room table. He clipped it to his nose and continued watching tennis on television.

WHEN I'M not looking, when my back is toward him, my husband hooks me around the neck with the crook of his cane and pulls me to him. We are so close, nothing can come between.

He props the cane against the counter. He turns me toward him, I enter his shadow, and we dance in place. I rest my head on his shoulder. We are old flames.

WE WALK in the woods, visiting our steadfast companions, the trees. We say hello to hackberry and Virginia pines. The close trees shatter sunlight into planes of various angles. If we look straight up, the sky recedes. Dragonflies hover on the verge of the gorge. Little Polecat Creek knows its place in the world and carries itself lightly. Deep inside the silence, we join hands and time passes, leaving us behind.

SOMETIMES HE goes to Raleigh or Greensboro or Meadows of Dan and leaves the dog and me behind. When he returns, our dog runs to greet him with a great gladness, long, floppy ears spread out like wings.

O MY HUSBAND; he is our spouse, brother to our hearts, our friend. We know we are his best beloveds.

WE ARE his home, it is we to whom he returns. When he is here time waits; time cools its heels.

A List of the Birds

MY SISTER is as sweet as clear water; she would bring us music: tambourines and flutes, the harp and the drum, her songs a brook rushing down a mountainside.

My sister has a tender heart, a heart that offers itself to others. For her, we will gather lilies and roses, and daisies and bachelor's button. Her eyes are like doves.

In our room at night I lie next to my husband and listen to his steady breathing. Our dog is asleep on the foot of the bed. I think about my sister, her stopped songs, her dove-soft eyes.

MOURNING DOVES, cardinals, goldfinches, phoebes, downy woodpeckers, hairy woodpeckers, red-bellied woodpeckers, a pair of pileated woodpeckers who live deep in the woods, yellow-bellied sapsuckers, summer tanagers, scarlet tanagers, green herons, great blue herons, the yellow-crowned night heron: all these have lighted on the feeder or dozed or trilled in trees or deliberated by the pond.

A FARMER's almanac: Winter snow settled on the tin roofs of the house, the barn, and the cottage, on the windowsills, on the bird feeder, in the bird bath. Mice scrabbled in the crawl space under the house. In spring the peepers sang hosannas from the pond. And in deep summer and early autumn, deer harvested apples, peaches, plums, taking them straight off the trees. The deer rear up on their hind legs and tug at the fruit and it seems to be a dance they are doing. My husband shot his rifle into the air. They fled to the woods, their scuts snapping to attention. Still later, red-berried nandina beside the house is a red mouth smiling. The purple tops of purple-top grass glow like a sunset that has slipped from the sky to the ground. October, now, and the day is windy, the bluebird house is empty. Time waits in the bushes and behind the trees.

I AM LOVED by my beloved; he is my spouse, my husband. He would have been a son to my parents, a brother to my brother.

Sometimes I can almost see them, my lost family, can almost see their faces in the clouds, hear their voices in the wind, father, mother, brother. At night they speak to me from the cave of the unconscious, but when I wake, their words are air and far away, drifting into cold, steep distance. *What? What did you say?* I almost remember, and always forget. It is like trying to catch snowflakes.

SNOWY EGRETS as serene and full of conviction as white-robed
Baptists waiting to be dunked, chipping sparrows, field sparrows, tree
sparrows, fox sparrows, white-throat sparrows, and swamp sparrows,
bluebirds, robins, and crows with murder on their minds and greed
in their throats: "My sisters the birds," St. Francis said, naming what
needs to be sung, and they are also ours.

ONE EARLY spring day, wind blustered into the laundry room and
knocked down a nest a pair of wrens had tucked into a pile of clothes.

They built another on a shelf over the washer and dryer, in the
lee of a big box of detergent, a bulwark against wild weather and wild
animals.

The female laid her eggs and brooded on them. During a cold
snap we ran the dryer over and over to help her keep the nest warm.
When the hatchlings emerged, we held a mirror up to the nest to see
them; their wide-open beaks seemed bigger than their bodies.

One evening we looked in on them and there, in the laundry
room, toddling wrens were trying out their wings, fledglings making
short hops from washer to clothes rack, long hauls from folding table
to open door to deck to low-branching shrub. Bits of down still stuck
to their crowns, poking straight up and making them all look like
Einstein.

I thought we would watch them grow, but my husband, who
knows these things, said, "They will be gone tomorrow."

Time has its way with the world.

DID WE HEAR the voice of the turtle then, in spring?

TIME MAKES memory possible; or memory makes time possible.

Time presents us with the past.

Time deprives us of the past.

Time protects us from the past.

Voices. Voices raised, then lowered. A comforting hand. I think
there was a comforting hand; it is not always easy to remember what

was real and what was wished for. But there was music, there was never a time without music.

Music describes the shape of time.

THE MUSIC of the hidden finds us out. In home or office, we hear the music we can't transcribe or score, the music of our living and our dying, and we dance until we dance no more.

MY HUSBAND says: "I am with you now."

WE HAVE also seen chickadees, juncos, warblers, winter and Carolina wrens, the red-breasted and the brown-headed nuthatch, a red-tailed hawk and a red-shouldered hawk, secretive flocks of strutting wild turkey, who see poorly at night, mockingbirds in maples, hummingbirds at the hummingbird feeder, meadow larks and blue jays, and quail and mallards and muscovys.

A guinea hen bobbles across the gravel drive and is lost in tall grass.

The strikingly beautiful but timid indigo buntings are growing bolder.

The American robin is really a thrush; the English robin is a robin.

In winter a cardinal in a cedar tree is a Christmas ornament.

Not seen but heard: owls and whippoorwills.

Storm

IT WAS A warm day, and the wind had a wildness to it. Taking our dog with him, my husband drove to town. I could smell his absence on the wind, and I hungered for him. I slipped on my skirt and a top the color of the sunflowers at field's edge and, for once, bedizened my feet with sandals.

The wind was like a spirit blowing over the grass. It bent the blades backward and forward. It made the purple-top grass sway like dancers.

I missed my husband's hand under my neck, his breath on my arms, his arms around me. I remembered his left hand under my neck, his right hand on my breast.

The wind pushed over a potted plant, a scatter of moist, dark soil on the deck. It blew my skirt against my legs. The sky was blue and the wind like ruffled feathers, and I felt something rough about the air, as if it might rip itself open.

AMONG THE trained steeds of Pharaoh, my husband would be like a wild horse, but here he is a roe or a hart that leaps (with a titanium hip).

We have a little sister. She is gentle and determined. She is small-boned and slender. She is as sweet as a rose of Sharon, and her heart is freely given.

CARDINALS AND goldfinches convened at the feeder. A wary bunting landed next to them. Picture them: pulsing blue, red, gold. When they flew, they were brooches on the breast of the sky. The day was windy, warm, purple-top grass swaying as if exercising in place, doing waist bends, turning side to side.

THE CAR with my spouse and our dog came up the dirt driveway. The dog was on my husband's lap, black nose out the window. The wind blew his rabbity ears flat against his small white head.

My heart raced out to greet them but I waited in the doorway, behind the screen door. Make haste, I thought; make haste.

OUR DOG is a white cloud on short, whirligig legs; my husband whistled, and he raced across the lawn, happy with a happiness too great to be named.

"HOW BEAUTIFUL are thy feet in shoes," my husband says as he comes in. And out he goes again, worms in hand, dog at heels, to fish for our supper.

I WENT OUT to search for him. Rain clouds were rolling in. I raced to the pond, the barn, the apple orchard, the edge of the woods. I called his name but he did not answer.

I returned to the house, cut off from my beloved.

Through the kitchen window, I see him make a stumbling run for the barn; he had gone down to his garden to bring in the mellow fruits of autumn. The white clouds have gathered their skirts and fled. The air has turned green. The birds have stopped singing; black clouds are massed overhead. The clouds' shadow swallows the lawn, the fields, the woods.

A pause, and then rain, hurled headlong down. Rain on tin roofs clatters like spilled nails. Branches crack, break, and fall. The lights go off. I am alone in the dark house while the air tears at itself. I look for candles but all I can find are ridiculous scented ones—ocean breeze, lavender, mulberry. We would prefer spikenard and saffron, calamus and cinnamon. We would prefer cluster of camphire.

The sky has dropped closer to the ground. Lightning fissures the sky and shreds the black clouds. Our windows are old, many panes loose or cracked, and the storm could knock them out and barge in.

I light the candles and listen to the storm in the highlighted dark. Boughs break and cradles fall. I remember that when my sister was six, she ran such a high fever we had to keep her awake all night in a bathtub filled with ice water. I remember the fear on my parents' faces. The nandina brushes the side of the house like a snare drum. The candles cast skinny, shimmering shadows on the walls. I remember the flush on my sister's face, the otherworldly look in her eyes, hectic and preoccupied. Water swirls along gutters and gushes out of the downspout. The house turns cool. Can a house harden its heart? The storm beats its head against the roof, the windows.

My husband and our dog wait out the storm in the barn.

While I am parted from him time weighs on me, a sadness bends my head.

When the rain stops, I step out onto the porch. A broadway of spider webs shines in the holly bush by the porch, each web a net with a catch of trembling raindrops.

Supper

THE SPIDER webs have slipped back into the part of the world that is hidden.

MAYFIELD FARM is rinsed and shining. We breathe in the deep-down freshness the poet sang. The air is at peace with itself. The sky has raised a clerestory opening onto an interior withheld from us. Mayfield's inhabitants come back out and show themselves in the open: Birds praise the clean air; monarchs renew their claim to the kingdom. We live in a green place, surrounded by elsewhere.

HOW DOES happiness happen? It happens in moments, in the interstices of hours and days. It happens at random, a mechanics of quanta, a principal uncertainty, without regard for what is earned or appropriate and not in keeping with the laws of physics as Newton knew them. It is both simpler and more mysterious than grace, which is given.

Or, how do we know that it does not happen all the time, day in and out, but we are not always in a place to experience it?

I REMEMBER a dark time and a cold place, but now I wonder, Was happiness there, and I failed to notice it? Was it there, and I unable to measure it? Was this rinsed world always waiting?

"A FROG-STRANGLER," my beloved said when he came in to change clothes. He kissed me and headed back out, to finish catching supper. He spends hours at the pond.

"Where is he?" people ask, when they call.

"He's down at the pond," I say.

Or "in the garden," I say, or "working out back," or, sometimes, "buying stuff."

"He'll be back soon," I say, and although I may wish it were sooner, he will return. He is my beloved and my friend; and I am his.

IF EVERYONE could be happy, and always, with a happiness too great to be named—

AS AFTERNOON declined, an odd creamy haze mottled the complexion of the sky—

UNTIL THE sun touched the treetops with flame and sparks flew to the roof, the porch, the deck, the chrysanthemums by the fence, the cropped tops of the boxwood, the hammock strung between trees. The purple-top grass was a field of candles, the flames rising and falling. The purple-top grass was feverish and trembling and then I watched the sky blue, the green of the cedar deepen, the windows cool; and the fever broke and the crisis was over.

THE CEDARS of Mayfield are as strong as love.

WE WILL sit down to our dinner of fish from the pond, fried sliced potatoes, and Swiss chard. The water in our water glasses will be ice-cold.

AS FOR happiness, as for happiness. . . . To be happy is to be seized by the day.

OUR SISTER will stay in the guest cottage, which will be finished by then, and it will be snug. If the wind picks up, the windows will hold tight against it. If the night is calm, she can hear the whippoorwills and owls, tree frogs and crickets. Clouds crossing the moon will throw moving shadows on the cottage floor. My husband builds well, lines plumb, angles exact. In the morning, she will look out on the fig tree that flares into a fan of branches at the low edge of the large southern window. She will stand on the screened porch that faces east.

"THE SPOON fell from my hand," she writes, in a letter that came today. "I could not reach to pick it up."

AT THE POND, in the garden, shopping, building, planting and weeding, fishing, my husband forgets what time it is.

Or time forgets itself, momentarily preoccupied as it is.

But he returns from his garden to his garden, from his bed of lilies to his bed of lilies, from waters that refresh to the waters that refresh.

Virginia Reel

IT WAS A windy day, warm for the season, the sky cerulean with cumulus clouds. Birds sang on the wing and in the trees. Squirrels chewed through twigs, flinging pecans onto the house's tin roof. Laundry line-danced in the wind. The potted plant on the deck turned over. My dark red hair snapped in the wind like a flag. I wore a long-sleeved pale yellow cotton top and a light blue skirt as soft as summer curtains. From the living-room window I saw a buck, and when I clapped my hands, he leapt out of the frame of the painting into the part of the world that is invisible. From the kitchen window, over the row of setting suns ripening on the sill, I saw fruit trees and the garden and green grass. The poplar leaves were like a metallic mobile, gold-leaf leaves spinning with pleasure. Purple-top grass shimmered, a field of bright haze shaking with laughter in the wind. It was only a day, but I wrote it down so I would not forget it. "Love is stronger than death," the singer says, but death is strong and rapacious. I have a sister I love. I love my husband. My husband and I have a little white dog. We love our dog, and he loves us. Butterflies and blue-tailed skinks, honey bees and marigolds, goldenrod in bloom, the chrysanthemums by the fence, the clouds and the reflections of clouds in the pond, the fish in the pond and the sun off the white car, the sweet gum and loblollies and Virginia pine, all are dancing, we are all dancing with the laundry and the purple-top grass and the wind chimes. Are we out of breath? Do our feet hurt? We'll sit out the next number; we'll watch the young take their turns. After a while we'll leave.

Four Kinds of Dark

THERE WAS A night in July. Beneath the moon the garden was green-blue, a stage-set. Deliquescent light on the oak limbs, the maple leaves; it was like a spilled liquid, but still: not flowing. The air was unmoving, burdened with damp. I heard a rustling in the forsythia, low, wondered were raccoons, possums, the huge orange tomcat who sometimes shows up foraging for food. The moon drew behind a cloud and the theater went black. The moon reappeared; and for a moment, a curtain was raised and the garden came back for an encore.

INSTEAD OF a brook rushing down a mountainside we have Little Polecat Creek, which travels a deep cut through secretive woods.

AT THE RIM of the sky darkness presses, a black arc, a curve like a snake or scrap of tire.

WE SHALL be pressed into the earth. Therein the darkness confounds. It estranges body from mind. Impenetrable, all-encompassing, it dissolves our limbs; our hands have been cut off, we cannot find our feet. We might go a little mad, wanting to touch every part of the body we think we own, but the mind refuses to be convinced. Only the darkness convinces. The mind, too, is dissolving, fluids and minerals leaking into the ground. How long ago were we overtaken? Who were we? There is no one to answer this question, just as there is no one to ask it. There is only the darkness.

WHAT CAN this mean? *Can* it mean?

MUST IT mean?

AND WHAT can we do for my sister? She has eyes like doves, and birds envied her songs, and we would keep her from harm.

WE WOULD but cannot, nor are there gods who will. Why not? we ask, but no one answers. The universe keeps secrets. What we know of it is only the surface. The far greater part of the universe is dark matter and dark energy. Dark matter is an unknown *somesuch* that can't be seen, in any light, by our eyes or our instruments. Dark energy, the force that drives all things, is the fundament; it is everywhere and inside us, and we know nothing about it. What we know is that, here in our lighted home, we live with darkness.

"TODAY I said absolutely nothing," my sister writes. "Time was too fast. I was too slow."

The Dance of Time

WE ARE the grass bowled over by the wind. In houses and meadows light comes and goes. "Stay," we say, but nothing does. Whose love is strong? Whose love can contend against the end of everything?

LIKE A stalking god the wind walked in the garden. Purple-top grass bowed and parted to make a path that closed as the god passed by. A small white dog chased squirrels. The sun was bright, the day unaccountably warm. Pecans and apples rained to the ground, harvesting themselves in their fullness. A great stag, foregrounded in the window frame, stared at me, his tarry gaze as obscure as the future. Cardinals in their red robes sang prayers. Chickadees tumbled from branch to twig, cheerful gymnasts in the cedar tree. My husband fired his rifle into the air, and the deer dissolved into the world of the hidden that is always near us.

IN A RAPTURE of attention, enrapt and attending, we slough off the sense of self; or shall we say, self is emptied out into soul. And what is soul? Soul is the shape of passion. It is the shape of that to which you have given yourself. When self is decanted into soul, self and soul become one. The plates of consciousness fit together perfectly. There might be music, given such harmony.

HERE IS the still point, the center that never changes, the singularity of the moment around which all things dance. We the dancers, the dancing, pirouette on the singularity's event horizon, held in place by its great gravity, which, like *caritas,* brings all things into relation with it. It is the singularity of the moment that lends to the dance the beauty of form, bringing order out of chaos.

IS A MOMENT too short? However short, the moment can be shorter. The moment is everywhere, and it is almost nowhere.

AT MAYFIELD, spacetime curves in upon itself and we are caught within. A day is an eternity though it lasts but a day. Scarlet tanagers drift among the branches of the pear tree. A raccoon climbs a ladder and watches me working in my second-floor study as if it has nothing better to do. My husband reads and goes fishing. Purple-top grass shimmies in the wind like a field of Shulamites.

WHO CALLS the dance? Or is there no call but from the stars, the wind, the birds in the birdbath, the foxes in the field, the hawk overhead, the dog wanting to be let out?

I HAVE A spouse, a partner. He is wise and silly. He comforts me with apples and makes me laugh. He is finishing the cottage for my sister. Hurry, I tell him. While we are here, we have much to do.

AS FOR OUR sister, we will welcome her with praise and honor her with wine, for she is brave and modest, bold and thoughtful, and she has made, of time, music.

HOLDING EACH other close, my husband and I dance in the kitchen. He is balm to my soul, a blessing upon my heart. He is my courage and my companion. I am his.

AT DUSK, from the screen porch, we listened to choirs of cicadas. Fireflies lit up the lawn erratically. Stars spangled the sky. Our planet, fateful and askew, cartwheels along its orbit. The rising moon, a jolly fellow, calls to us, tugs at our watery bodies. I thought of my family, who call to me in my dreams. A bat brushed against the sky, like a hand of God.

MY HUSBAND and I and our dog climbed the stairs to our bedroom. The south-facing window disclosed scrapings of shadow against shadow as the loblollies pitched and swayed in the wind. The fireplace mantel held a vase of Dijon yellow and the vase held a spray of dark red sumac. I helped our dog onto the high bed; he moved to the bottom, curled into himself, and was instantly asleep. My husband and I slipped under the lightweight patchwork quilt. My husband turned on his side and I lay beside him. My body grew warm in the scallop of his. We sleep in the lee of the slanted ceiling, sheltered like dozing wrenlets. From time to time some creature—deer, cat, skunk, rabbit— sets off the flood light sensor and light bursts into the bedroom, a slam of light, and, moments later, withdraws, leaving us in the dark.

HURRY, MY LOVE. While we are here, we have much to do.

Night is on its way. Before anything changes, make haste, my beloved, and I will be your orchard of delights.

NOTES

The "Songs for a Soviet Composer" were written for the Latvian composer Imants Kalniņš. At the time, Latvia was under Soviet domination. In 1991, Latvia reclaimed its status as an independent nation.

"A Scientific Expedition in Siberia, 1913" is dedicated to the memory of my father, J. Milton Cherry, who contributed to it the name "Szymanowski," borrowed from the Polish composer Karol Szymanowski (1882–1937).

In "Requiem," the "line by Christopher Marlowe" alluded to can be found in his *Tragical History of Doctor Faustus:* "See, see where Christ's blood streams in the firmament!"

ACKNOWLEDGMENTS

The author would like to thank the editors of the following publishing houses, who printed the books in which these poems first appeared. From *Lovers and Agnostics* (Carnegie Mellon University Press, 1995; first published by Red Clay Books, 1975): "The Bride of Quietness," "Death Comes to Those Who Know It."

From *Relativity: A Point of View* (Carnegie Mellon University Press, 2000; first published by Louisiana State University Press, 1977): "Dora," "Fission," "Lt. Col. Valentina Vladimirovna Tereshkova," "My Marriage," "The Pines without Peer," "She Goes to War."

From *Natural Theology* (Louisiana State University Press, 1988): "At Night Your Mouth," "The Family," "Forecast," "How to Wait," "Ithaca," "Late Afternoon at the Arboretum," "The Lonely Music," "Natural Theology," "Paranoia," "Questions and Answers," "The Rose," "A Scientific Expedition in Siberia, 1913."

From *God's Loud Hand* (Louisiana State University Press, 1993): "At a Russian Writers' Colony," "Berlin: An Epithalamion," "Family Life in the Twentieth Century," "Galilee," "Golgotha," "Grace," "The Heart of the World," "History," "In the End," "Looking Back," "Love," "Memory," "Now the Night," "The Promise," "The Radical," "The Raiment We Put On," "Reading, Dreaming, Hiding," "Report from an Unnamed City," "The Same Rose," selections from "Songs for a Soviet Composer," "And Then," "Waiting for the End of Time," "Woman Living Alone," "Work."

From *Death and Transfiguration* (Louisiana State University Press, 1997): "The Almost-Baby," "Alzheimer's," "Anniversary," "A Diminishing Chord Modulating into Nihilism," "Epithalamium," "Falling," "First Marriage," "From Venice: Letter to an Ex-Husband," "How We Are Taken," "Imagining the Past," "Miracle and Mystery," "My Mother's Swans," "On Looking at an Artwork by My Ex-Husband, after His Death," "Prayer for My Father: In Memoriam," "Requiem."

From *Rising Venus* (Louisiana State University Press, 2002): "Adult Ed. 101: Basic Home Repair for Single Women," "Bat Mother," "Catching Hell," "The Grecian Grace of a White Egret," "The Horse at Dusk," "Lady Macbeth on the Psych Ward," "Man on the Hall," "My House," "Nobody's Fool," "On Looking at a Yellow Wagon," "An Other Woman," "Rising Venus," "Study for an Annunciation," "Sunrise," "To a Young Woman," "Virgin and Child," "Wishing I Could Bring You Back and See Things More Clearly This Time Around."

"In the Field" first appeared, in an earlier version, in *Agni* (1990). "Wild Dogwood" first appeared, in an earlier version, in *Appalachian Heritage* (2004). An excerpt from "Virginia Reel" appeared in *Atlanta Review* (2004). "The Heat Down South (Richmond, 1955)" first appeared in *Comstock Review* (2006). "God in the South" first appeared, in an earlier version, in *Image* (1999). "Byrd's Survey of the Boundary: An Abridgment" first appeared in *Parting Gifts* (1993). My thanks to the editors of the foregoing journals. Thanks also to the Virginia Center for the Creative Arts for residencies during which I worked on this book (2003, 2004). Heartfelt thanks to the Humanities Center, the English Department, and the College of Liberal Arts at the University of Alabama in Huntsville for great colleagues, for dialogue across disciplines, and for general all-around friendliness. Thanks, most especially, to Louisiana State University Press for thirty years of editorial guidance, superb production values, and a capable, good-natured, and caring staff in all areas and their unfailing dedication to literature.

To R. H. W. Dillard: big hug.